STORIES FROM A BLUE BAG

In the Beginning There Was Creativity (layered print)

STORIES FROM A BLUE BAG

A Memoir

Karl J. Volk

Epigraph Books
Rhinebeck, New York

Paperback ISBN 978-1-951937-91-1
Hardcover ISBN 978-1-951937-92-8
eBook ISBN 978-1-951937-93-5

Library of Congress Control Number 2020925868

All art work depicted in this memoir is the work of Karl J. Volk, except for the depictions of the Schloss Johannisburg in Chapters 11 and 13.
- The artist and maker of the plate on page 61 is unknown.
- The banknote on page 68 incorporated a painting by Adalbert Wilheim Hock.

All photographs are part of Karl J. Volk's personal family collection of photographs or postcards, except those listed below. The names of the studios in which some photos were taken are unknown.
- The photograph of the Karl J. Volk in "About the Author" taken at Vassar College Campus in Spring of 2020, by Laura Ann Garzilli Bracken.
- SS Breman photo by Bundesarchiv, Bild 102-11081 / Georg Pahl / CC-BY-SA 3.0, CC BY-SA 3.0 de, https://commons.wikimedia.org/w/index.php?curid=5415237

Book design by Colin Rolfe

Epigraph Books
22 East Market Street, Suite 304
Rhinebeck, NY 12572
(845) 876-4861
epigraphps.com

Dedication:

This book is dedicated to my mother, Emily Volk,
who made the blue bag
out of which my stories grew.

Thank You:

I would like to thank Laura A.G. Bracken
for the enormous amount of work she did to pull this book together.
It would not have happened without her.

Praising the Sun (watercolor, pen, and collage)

Blovel Root (watercolor)

CONTENTS

INTRODUCTION

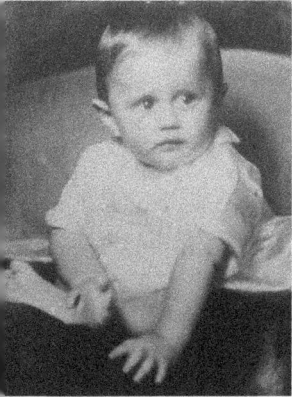

This is me as a baby, not long before I was sent away.

T HESE "Blue Bag Stories" are about my life, starting as an eleven-month-old baby sent to Germany in 1933. I was sent away because the Great Depression affected my parents to the point where they could not cope with a baby in their lives. The stories are about my life in Germany as well as my life once I returned to the United States, as a fourteen-year-old, in 1946. At this point, I spoke only German, and I was meeting my parents for the first time.

While in Germany, I lived in a small village called Holzkirchhausen with my uncle Ottmar and my aunt Karolina. I also lived part of that time in the medium-sized city of Aschaffenburg with my uncle Otto and my aunt Lizzy. There, we were bombed by English and American planes. Throughout this time, I was exposed to many atrocities of the National Socialist Party and their leader, Adolf Hitler, including seeing a train of Jews being taken to a concentration camp. Some of these stories are not easy to read but should be known. The title of the book refers to my mother, Emily Volk, and the blue shoulder bag she sewed for me that I wore for many years.

Mullen on Blue (monoprint)

MY PARENTS

M Y parents immigrated to the United States in the early part of the twentieth century. They came from two different countries and did not know each other before arriving here. My father came first, from a little village called Holzkirchhausen in western Bavaria. That part of Bavaria was really Franconia. It was given to Bavaria by Napoleon, making Bavaria a kingdom. The dialect of this area was different from that of Bavaria proper. I may occasionally use dialect words, just to show the reader how it is different from High German. Nowadays, the dialect is virtually gone. It was forbidden by the Bavarian education department sometime around the year 2000, on the grounds that the children might become confused in school between the dialect and High German. The government even forbade the parents from speaking the dialect to their children. When I found out about this, I was appalled that a government would do such a thing! I had spoken this dialect as

My parents: Emily Volk and Karl Alfons Volk.

my first language and had also learned High German in school, as did all the other kids going to school at that time.

My mother came from an even smaller village called Podpreska, in an area that is now part of Slovenia. She also grew up bilingual. She could speak Slovenian (which is a mix of Slavic and Latin) and a Germanic dialect she called *Gottscheberisch*, which is now, according to Wikipedia in quoting UNESCO, a "critically endangered language." You see, when she was born, the area that is now Slovenia was part of the Austro-Hungarian Empire. So at that time, many people from different areas could move into different language realms but still be in the same political country. Gottscher was the German name of her area.

Today, Slovenians call that area Cojevia. The Roman Emperors had built palaces there, especially on the Croatian coast. Podpreska, however, was a tiny, backwoods village, and the house where my mother was born became intolerable to her.

My mother was baptized as Amalia Turk. She was born into a family that was healthy until her mother contracted tuberculosis and eventually died from it. After that, and apparently even before her mother's death, her father, Ivan Turk, courted a widow with five children. Before much time had elapsed after his first wife's death, this widow moved into my mother's house with her five children, where the five children—my mother and her siblings—already lived. The offspring of the first wife were furious! If any problems occurred among the many children, it was always the fault of the first brood. Mary, mother's older sister, managed to find money somehow to emigrate to the United States where she found as a maid for a Jewish household in Brooklyn.

As soon as she could, Mary sent money to my mother to buy a ticket to immigrate to Brooklyn as well. My mother also became a maid, in three private households, and paid off her debt to Mary. She in turn sent money to Anna, her younger sister, who left for western Canada. She was a mail-order bride to a Slovenian man who had become a miner out there. Anna later told me it was a very long train ride to get there.

My mother's brother, Ivan, stayed in Slovenia, which eventually became a part of Yugoslavia. During the time of Yugoslavian president Josip Broz (commonly known as "Tito"), many German speakers, mostly from Austria, were evicted from communist Yugoslavia on the grounds that they had cooperated with the Nazis. Ivan became a forester under Tito and moved around a lot and had a number of children. One of them, Antun Turk, was also an artist, and was elected mayor of a small Croatian city.

When my mother was not busy working and learning English, she attended dances. My mother used to tell me that she would go to dances in the Yorkville section of Manhattan, now known as the Upper East Side, in a large German community where German was spoken and dances were held. I assume that's how they met. This is where she met my father, and eventually, they decided to get married. I know nothing of their courtship, but they probably discussed the possibility of opening a butcher shop, as that was the trade my father had learned in Germany. I believe that since he would not farm and most of the land would go to his brother Ottmar, he received some money to pay for learning a trade. He did, however, acquire some land located in the outskirts of Hausa. It included a field as well as woodland. My mother was paid a small sum for this after World War II ended, and I had returned to the United States.

My sister, Helen, was four-and-a-half years older than me. She was born on January 19, 1928. Since my parents had been married only seven months before, on June 19, 1927, my mother was very likely pregnant with her at the time. I remember seeing a photograph with my mother in a bridal outfit. The photo was taken by a professional photographer in sepia tones. Sometime in the 1950s, I got to meet their best man and his wife while they still lived in New York City. They later moved to Connecticut, and I lost track of them.

MY TRIP TO GERMANY IN 1933

,

T HE height of the Great Depression was in 1932, so my arrival on August 15th of that year was a bit of a disaster for my mother. By that time, she had changed not only her last name, but also her first. She was now known as Emily. She must have done that during the wedding preparations. According to her, my father was not a good businessman, for he gave credit when he should not have done so. Their customers, who needed food but did not have much money, tried to get as much as possible for every penny. If they owed too much money, they would just go to another store and do the same thing there. They did not pay their bills at all, which was very bad for business. If you appeared kind, you were taken advantage of, and the news traveled fast. This store was located at 725 Lewis Avenue in the Bedford-Stuyvesant neighborhood of Brooklyn.

This neighborhood was then a virtually all-black neighborhood, and people bought the cheapest cuts of meat. Pig tails, hog maws, and chitterlings, as well as smoked ham hocks, were common purchases. It became a problem to pay the electric bill. There was a walk-in freezer, a show case, and overhead lights. Then there was me, Karl Joseph Volk, to feed. This meant my mother could not always prevent my father from allowing people to charge their bill instead of paying with cash. My mother thought if she could go to work, the store could be saved. Work was hard to get, but mother told me many times that she had the most gorgeous hair and a great figure, and Macy's had promised her a job. I had to go for this tight economic ploy.

An additional consideration for my being sent away was the fact that my sister became afflicted with polio about the time of my birth, causing her to be quarantined for a period of time. Ultimately, one of her legs would always be shorter than the other. Though my father attempted to prevent me from being sent away, mother won the battle. Her ultimatum was that if I were not sent away, she would take Helen away with her and leave me with him. This he could not deal with, so arrangements were made that I would be taken to the next boat leaving for Germany. That boat was the SS Bremen.

SS Bremen.

*Mama Karolina and Uncle Ottmar's
wedding portrait.*

THIS story is about the person who raised me from age eleven months to age fourteen years. As you know, my mother, Emily Volk, who had given birth to me in Kings County Hospital on August 15, 1932, sent me to Germany on the SS Bremen. The nurse and sailors took care of me until my arrival in Bremen, Germany. I don't have any recollection of that time.

I am sure that my mother informed Ottmar and Karolina by letter of my arrival as close to the day on which it might happen. Transatlantic cables had been laid by that time to facilitate the transport of urgent information across oceans. At any rate, Karolina had to travel from tiny Holzkirchhausen in western Bavaria to the far-away city of Bremen on the North Sea. It was a problem just to get to Würzburg. Würzburg was only twenty-five kilometers away, but there was no public transportation between there and Holzkirchhausen. In Würzburg she would have been able to get on a train. It is highly likely that she had never taken a train ride before in her life. At that time, peasant farmers just never traveled anywhere. They were tied to their land and their village. There was so much work to be done each day; travel was not on the menu.

Somehow, Mama Karolina had to rise to the occasion to manage this trip. I would not be surprised if it took more than one day. At any rate, it was a long and tiring trip. Karolina might have been to Würzburg once before on a pilgrimage to the Käppele, a trip that was encouraged by the church and the community. This trip was usually done on foot. The Käppele is a beautiful chapel on one of several mountains that surround Würzburg. One of the other mountains supported the *Festung*, a huge castle that once housed the overlords of the city. The sides of these mountains are planted with wine grapes, which produce the wine for which the city was, and still is, famous.

Karolina holding me as a toddler.

Würzburg sits at the river *Main* (the longest tributary of the Rhine), in a beautiful setting with many architectural marvels, the greatest of which is the *Residenz*, with ceiling murals by Giovanni Tiepelo, a grand staircase, and beautiful baroque gardens.

On this trip, Mama Karolina could not be sidetracked by any of this as she had so many things on her mind. She must have thought of having diapers and a milk bottle for when she would finally arrive in Bremen. How would she carry me along with a suitcase and food? Would I need to be bathed on the train, and how would she manage that—there or at the hotel? I wonder if she arrived several days ahead of time to make sure she was there when the ship arrived.

While I was growing up under her care, I did not know that she had single-handedly done all that to bring me to her house in tiny Holzkirchhausen. And I did not know that I was not her birth child for many years.

I remember seeing a small black-and-white photo of Karolina standing next to Ottmar at the northeast corner of the building that housed the *Gasthaus zum Grünen Baum*, where I grew up. I had not yet arrived in that photo, and it was probably taken not that long after they were married. I had also seen their wedding photos, one of which appears above. Ottmar and Karolina never produced any children of their own. In her wedding photo she was wearing a black dress and a white veil. Perhaps someone in her family had died. She always wore her hair in a braided knot at the back of her head. In the fields, she always wore a kerchief. They were either white with black polka dots or deep blue with white polka dots. She worked very hard in the fields, in the garden, and in the house.

Mama Karolina's maiden name was Luder, as she told me once when I was old enough to ask such questions. And I remember I laughed because *luder* in German is a female who is not a very nice person. She also had a stepsister named Klothilda, who lived up the street from us. In Klothilda's house also lived their father, who was by then a fairly old man. So naturally, I assumed him to be my grandfather. In that area of Bavaria, the Franconian dialect was spoken and grandfather was *Herrla*. That came from the German word *Herrlein*, which means "little mister." The suffix *lein* is a form of endearment, but it means smaller or makes a word diminutive. And grandmother was called *Fräla*, which I write more about in Chapter 4.

When Fräla became bedridden, Herrla would frequently take me off Mama Karolina's hands and move me about in a little children's wagon. This way he did not have to carry me but could still take me along on the errands he had to do. While Klothilda's husband, Lorenz, was still in the village, he did most of the farm labor, but as the war went on, he, along with many other peasant farmers, was called to the front. This made the life of the farm women extremely difficult.

The absence of able-bodied men to work the fields led the National Socialists to bring in people from conquered areas to do the work that simply could not have been accomplished without their slave labor, which is how we obtained a French prisoner of war. The sowing and reaping had to continue at all costs to keep the country and the German army supplied with food. This was also a reason that boys had to take on the labor that their fathers would have done, as soon as possible. Uncle Ottmar, too, was called up, but he was never sent to the front. Instead, he was sent to Kitzingen, which is a bit east of Würzburg and could be reached by train from there. At one point in the fall, when most of the farm work had been done, Mama Karolina took me with her to visit him in the *Kaserne* where he was stationed. A Kaserne was the barracks and buildings where soldiers were trained. We brought apples for Ottmar, which he naturally shared with the other soldiers there.

Uncle Ottmar (standing) and other soldiers enjoying the apples we brought them in their Kaserne at Kitcingen.

At that time, there was a way to be driven to the train station. A man had bought a small bus and, for a fee, would drive you into the city. This method of transportation must have been used by Mina, the sister of Hans. Hans worked on the farm while Ottmar was in the military. Hans lived in Würzburg and working on the land gave him food for himself and his relatives. Mina worked mostly in the house, whereas Karolina worked mostly in the fields with the slaves, Fritz and Baraska, whom

I talk about in more detail in later chapters. And as soon as I was old enough and able to help out, I was also taken to the fields.

My first job that I could remember was to help with the potato harvest. The simplest of the tasks was to gather the potatoes into the willow baskets that Ottmar had made. The filled baskets were then emptied into sacks. I held the sacks open while others poured the potatoes into them. That part was tricky as the potatoes could easily fall to the sides, which made more work. After a while, my little hands were coated with soil from the newly-harvested potatoes. This soil made my hands feel very uncomfortable and dried out. Hard cider and seltzer water, which had been brought along, never tasted that good again in later life.

Mama Karolina coaxed me along in my labor and encouraged me with promises of special foods she knew I liked, pancakes being one of them. She would make huge ones in a large pan on a wood fire. I carried the wood in from the woodshed on the north side of the building, or from stacks out in the open. Later, when I lived in Aschaffenburg, I missed those pancakes and the next day's pancake soup, but I was glad to have left the fields behind.

4

MY FATHER'S FAMILY:
PHILLIP, APOLONIA AND THEIR SONS

This is me with Fräla, my Grandmother Apolonia.

MY father, Karl Alfons Volk, was one of five brothers born to Phillip and Apolonia Volk. Phillip, my paternal grandfather, had been married before, but his first wife had died in childbirth, and he was hard-pressed to quickly find another mother for his daughter. In order to do this, concerned locals helped him put out a newspaper ad, to which Apolonia Ott responded. At the time, Apolonia was working as a cook in a monastery across the Main *Fluss* (river) from Miltenberg. She had been born in Reichartshausen in the Odenwald region of Germany.

Because of the urgency with which Phillip had to find a new wife and mother to his infant child, Apolonia was quite prepared to make stipulations, even though she was a good cook and the monks did not want her to go. She devised, perhaps with help from one of the monks, a plan that she would marry Phillip only if her domestic duties were limited. Her prenuptial agreement (very forward-looking and unusual for that time, especially in a peasant farm village) stated that she would only work in the house and garden; she would not work in the stables nor the fields; she would serve beer in the restaurant, cook meals, and take care of the child (who sadly would pass early on), among other stipulations. Phillip, in his need to get someone to take care of his baby girl and the house, accepted the stipulation.

This arrangement worked out well and kept Apolonia from being overworked as so many other women were. Still, there was a great deal to do because not only were there the fields and animals, there was also the *Wirtschaft*, also called the *Gasthaus*. A "Wirtschaft" was like a small pub, but there was not an actual bar at which to drink. Instead, men and women ordered their beverages from a table, and the drinks were brought to them. A "Gasthaus" is also like that, but in addition, people are able to spend the night there.

Three of Father's brothers, Mama Karolina, and me (in the middle) with two cousins.

Since Holzkirchhausen was a village of about 300 people, and everyone was a peasant farmer, there was not much time for beer drinking. Men and women were preoccupied with sowing and reaping their crops and feeding their cows and pigs. That included keeping the stables as clean as possible, which was a lot of work in itself. The manure of the pigs and cows, which were kept in the stables, had to be brought by hand to a pile of stinking manure which was outside every kitchen in the village. *Mistsudel*, the liquid remains, were stored underground until it was time to pump them up into wooden or metal containers that lay on top of wooden wagons. After the container was full, the cows and/or a horse pulled this load to a field where it was sprayed onto the soil. At other times, on other wagons, the solid manure was piled on and brought to the fields. This work was incredibly difficult—to pull the manure off the wagons and then spread it over the soil. It had to be done at specific times before crops were sown or after they had been harvested. The manure was plowed under to enrich the soil for the next season's sowing.

Although Apolonia was saved from all of this, she was still busy sowing two gardens where vegetables were grown not only for the present, but also to preserve for the winter. Preserving cabbage is how Germany got to be famous for its sauerkraut. I remember how preserving vegetables was a big job involving countless details that had to be managed.

Apolonia was soon pregnant with her firstborn, Otto. Later in his life, he was allowed to be educated. He studied French and English and eventually became a teacher of these languages at a teacher preparatory school in Aschaffenburg, where I would eventually live with him and his wife Lizzy. Lizzy's maiden name was Grobholz and she was from Pirmasens, near the western border of Germany with France.

The reason for sending Otto to school was that there was simply not enough arable land to allow all the boys of the family to become peasant farmers. Heinrich, the third son, was able to stay in the village because he married a woman who had inherited some land of her own. Heinrich also received some land from his father. Heinrich raised his family in the house that his wife inherited. He had a family of five children. There were four boys and the youngest child was a girl named Ida.

The second Volk son, Gustave, was in the First World War and died there. His name appears in the little chapel by the cemetery on the hill south of Holzkirchhausen. The graves in the cemetery are beautifully kept with seasonal and perennial flowers and hedges. The red sandstone Stations of the Cross, which were a gift from one of the families of the village, are within sight, across the road to the next town south, Neubrunn. They were previously shaded by enormous horse chestnut trees until it became obvious the shade was bad for the sculpted sandstone of the Stations. The trees were cut down in favor of protecting the stone sculptures. I still grieve for these trees under which I used to play as a child. In Germany graves are only kept for twenty-five years

STORIES FROM A BLUE BAG

unless they are repurchased. There is just not enough land to expand the cemeteries.

The fourth boy born to Apolonia was my father, Karl Alfons Volk. I have seen a head shot of him when he was about twenty-years old. He appears in a group photo in a uniform. The photo is located in the local *Heimatmuseum*—a kind of museum dedicated to the unique German concept of *heimat*, a form of local cultural identity—which was created in about 2010 when Reiner Volk (not immediately related) agreed to become its administrator. It is also the former Kindergarten, which was created by the National Socialists while I was growing up in the village between 1933 and 1946, with intervals in Aschaffenburg.

MAP OF HOLZKIRCHHAUSEN

14

The fifth and last boy to be born to my grandparents was Ottmar, who inherited the home building and the wirtschaft called *Zum Grünen Baum*.

Apolonia, like all other old ladies of Holzkirchhausen, wore long skirts all the way to the floor. And there seemed to be several layers of them. They seemed to be all of a dark color. An apron with a loop around the neck completed the outfit. Her hair, like that of all the other old ladies, was worn in a braided bun high on the back of the head. When she went to church, she, like all other Frälas, wore only black.

I remember when I was very small, Apolonia would bake many loaves of bread in the large oven that was situated in the north wall of the kitchen. She had a long-handled wooden ladle with which she could push in and retrieve the large loaves from the fire when they were baked. She made sure I was far away from there. She said sternly, "Stay over there and don't come any closer." At that time she was quite old already and Phillip had died. The oven was removed soon after she was no longer able to manage the difficult task of using it. That space became part of the restaurant section of the building.

As I mentioned earlier, I did not call Apolonia by that name, of course. She was my grandmother. In that part of Germany, which was a part of Franconia, people spoke the Franconian dialect, which varied slightly from village to village. The name I called her, "Fräla," comes from the High-German word *"Fräulein,"* which means unmarried woman. "Fräulein" is no longer used today, for is now considered a slur word, as it demeans being unmarried. It's sort of how people used to be called "Old Maid" in our country. All adult women are now called *Frau*, and grandmothers are now called *"Oma."*

One day when I was still very small, I witnessed something terrible that happened to my Fräla. We were in the kitchen together, and in the kitchen, the floor was made of cement with tiny stones embedded. It was a very hard floor. She was washing dishes in the big cement *guss* (a type of sink) and had to move something she had washed. However, she had to step down in order to do this, and perhaps because the area around the sink was wet, she missed the step and fell very hard onto the floor. I was terrified, but soon I realized she needed help. So I ran outside to tell Mama Karolina, who was in the barn. After she came into the house, she gave me a task or an errand to do, so I would be out of the way while she called for more people to help. The next time I saw Apolonia again she was in bed—where, sadly, she stayed for the rest of her life.

Woman Knitting (pastel)

5

MY EARLY YEARS IN HOLZKIRCHHAUSEN

Gruß aus Holzkirchhausen

A T my arrival in Holzkirchhausen (*Hausa*, for short) in 1933, I was nearly a year old, because It was late July or early August when I arrived. Ottmar's wife, Karolina, had gone to Bremen to pick me up from the ship.

Karolina, being the wife of a peasant farmer, was a very busy person, having to work both in the fields and the house. Fräla Apolonia was still alive at this point, and this was a great help to Karolina, because Fräla did a lot of the cooking. As I explained before, Karolina's father, Herrla, would pull me around in a little four-wheeled cart.

There were also girls who lived diagonal from where I lived with Ottmar, Karolina, and Apolonia. I was likely given to these girls when Karolina was working in the fields and no one else was free to take care of me. My body, not so much mind, remembers being dropped by one of these girls, who were sisters. At some point, the red sandstone steps where I had been dropped were pointed out to me. To this day, I have a dent in my head. I do remember crying a lot and the girls screaming at each other as to whose fault it was. That may have been the reason Karolina called on her father to pull me around in that little wagon.

The National Socialist Party, also know as the Nazi Party, had come into power at that time. People had taken sides. Ottmar was a party member, and Karolina was not. Because he was a party member, Ottmar became mayor. He was able to procure for me a beautiful rocking horse. There are photos of me on it in front of the barn doors. Many years later, I saw it again after it had been ruined, and I felt sad.

Ottmar, I was later told by my cousin Dr. Matthias Haber, lost the title of mayor when he did not approve of the way the Jews were treated.

I lach neet.

I remember the time he had Jews from a nearby village sit in the *Stüble* (a small guest room), where they had mugs of beer.

Karolina objected to the Nazi development. The fact that she would have preferred to display the Bavarian, blue-and-white flag, rather than the Swastika, indicates that. I have no memory of what she said about all of this, but the facial expressions she made gave me a clue to her feelings.

At some point, Uncle Otto, the oldest brother of my father, and his wife Lizzy came to visit, and during the visit a cute photo was taken of me looking very grim, with the arm of *Tante* (Aunt) Lizzy visible. On the back of the photo was written "*I lach neet,*" which means "I won't laugh." I had a little beret on, as well as an apron, short pants, and a scowl. My arms were crossed as Tante Lizzy attempted to cajole me to play along for the camera. All boys in Germany at that time wore short pants and stockings all year long. In the summer, one might have worn socks or knee stockings, and in the winter, long stockings held up with rubber bands. This went on until the age of eighteen. Aprons for little boys in the villages were very common. They were easy to wash and pants were not!

This photo shows a street view of the village. I still wouldn't laugh.

While Karolina was not a Nazi Party member, and had a negative attitude towards them, she did appreciate two benefits that came from them. One was the kindergarten, and the other was the bath, which was added in back of the kindergarten building. The fact that the kindergarten was only on the other side of her garden on the north side of the house made this especially handy. It was a great relief for her to have me in a safe place for several hours a day when she could work in the fields without worrying about me. This was 1936, and I was four. The kindergarten teacher was a party member, which had helped her get the job. She was not from the village but came from another part of Germany. She did have a young paid helper from the village named Rösla. Rösla came from the family that ran the post office right next to and south of the huge Linden Tree in the center of the village.

Mama Karolina was so glad there was now a way to have a warm bath, and that it was nearby. When she planned to take a bath she had to make sure someone was scheduled to start the stove that heated the water, and that no one else had already secured that time slot. There were only two tubs and two showers, and there were 350 residents in the village. When she went to bathe there she was able to take me with her so I could take a shower. The water was heated with wood and coal. The heating was done in a room adjacent to the actual bath area. I do not know if the people stoking the fire were volunteers or were paid by the village. This method of heating water is quite time consuming.

None of the houses had hot showers built in. Some of these houses were built in the 1600s. Every tiny amount of water had to be heated on an old-fashioned wood stove in the kitchen. There, people might have set up a large tin bowl in front of a chair, where they would sit with their feet in the water. Then, to wash the rest of the body, you stood up and used a washcloth. Hair was washed in the kitchen sink before or after you washed your body. The rest of the family had to wait in another room until each person had their turn, or they often went without a wash.

In the winter, the stove had to be kept going since there was no other heat anywhere in the house, unless you also had a wood stove in the living room. For the bed, you could have tin bed warmers or ceramic bottles filled with hot water. Most often you had to go into a cold bed.

For these reasons, laundry was also a huge problem. Since there were no dryers, people waited for spring to do large laundry days. I remember Uncle Ottmar's socks were thrown into a small cupboard under the stairs for months at a time until the season was just right to do laundry. On those days, the huge kettle was brought out from storage and wood and coal was brought to the kettle. A smoke stack was fastened to the kettle to direct the smoke out of the range of the eyes. If the wind co-operated, you could approach the kettle without tears in your eyes. All of this had to be carefully planned ahead of time, when one expected a sunny day so the laundry could dry on lines that had been set up at least a day ahead of time. These lines were strung up on the north side of the barn, where the woodshed was attached. The lines started there and went from tree to tree until all of them had been used up.

* * *

THE ground was the home of the chickens. A fence kept them within their area and out of the garden. The chickens roosted in a small building, north of the area where the laundry was hung. There was a chicken-sized door for the chickens and a human-sized door for the humans to enter to collect eggs, which was one of my jobs. I also fed the chickens. When I was a little older, I cleaned the pigsties and dragged the manure over to the manure pile. New straw was then put in each sty. During the cleaning, the pigs were allowed to roam on the large manure pile. They loved being out of their confining, dark sties, and their movements compacted the manure.

During the potato harvest, I helped collect the potatoes and put them into bags. Others loaded the bags onto the wagon. At the house, the potatoes were allowed to roll into the cellar under the house via a chute through the cellar window. In the cellar, another person had to distribute them more evenly. My hands got pretty rough from this type of work. There was also a lot of walking done from the house to the fields and back home again. When it was possible to ride on a wagon pulled by cows or a horse, one took a ride. At some point after the war started, it was rumored that Americans were dropping potato beetles. Whether or not this was true is hard to say, but in any case, there were a lot of beetles, and we had to walk out to the fields to collect the various stages of this beetle. The eggs were the hardest to see because they were often under the leaf. The village sometimes organized the residents to go out in large groups to make sure this task was not neglected by any individual peasant farmer.

Such events were announced by one of the sisters of the family that operated the post office. They came through the streets ringing a loud bell. This caused people to open their windows to listen to the announcements. The sisters would also announce local news and when people were to assemble for longer news or labor that had to be done for the common good. If a street had to be repaired, villagers had to hammer large stones into smaller pieces, and load these into wagons. And someone had to volunteer their animals to pull the wagons to the site where the stones were needed. Perhaps the bathing times were also announced by the girls.

* * *

BECAUSE of my small size, I was kept in the kindergarten a year longer

Me and some neighborhood friends playing atop some lumber in front of my kindergarten.

than the others, who went on to first grade in the *Volkschule* (elementary school), which was the large red sandstone building next to the Linden Tree. My age group moved up in September 1937, after we had had our fifth birthdays. I did not get to first grade until September 1938, when I was six years old.

When I got to first grade, we sat in the very front of the room. In the winter, this room was heated by a large iron stove. The eighth grade sat at the very rear, in larger seats, and the windows behind them overlooked the Linden Tree. We had one teacher for all grades, so it was a bit confusing sometimes as to which group the teacher was addressing. The first grade learned the letters of the alphabet. The letters we learned were the old Germanic forms, not the Roman alphabet, which we learned later. As soon as we had mastered the Germanic alphabet, we were given our first reader.

At this point, Adolph Hitler had been in power for several years, but now he was a dictator known as *der Führer* (the leader), and no one was able to contradict him in any way. On the first page of our reader, there was a flag with a swastika on it, and a little girl and boy were standing underneath it with their arms raised in the Hitler salute. The words *Heil Hitler* stood in black letters on the page. I do not recall much else about this book, just that it was a thin book. The teacher we started with soon disappeared and a new teacher, who was a party member, took over.

I stayed in this school for about two years. During this time, Uncle Ottmar and Uncle Otto must have discussed when I would be moving to

Aschaffenburg. Also during this time, we had a French prisoner of war working for us. These prisoners were housed at night in one of the oldest houses in the village. On Sundays I was asked to bring food to our French man at this house. I saw that there were bunk beds. There was a strong male smell in the room when I handed the food over. Apparently, the French could receive packages from home, which I know because I recall getting a small piece of chocolate from one of them. By this time, chocolate could not be found in German stores.

Our prisoner had a problem. I saw him grabbing himself in the groin as he was pitching unthreshed grain bundles up to the second story of the barn. I knew that he was in pain. He did not know that I could see him from the kitchen window while he was on a wagon in the barn some distance away. I told Uncle Otto, who was visiting at the time, because I knew he could speak French, and I was concerned for the man. I did not think he should be doing that kind of work if he was ill. I had heard of such problems from conversations I had overheard in the guest rooms, where we served beer. Uncle Otto was uncomfortable talking to the man about this subject. I could tell by his voice and body language. He kept

Our draft horse with one of the French prisoners of war who worked for us.

STORIES FROM A BLUE BAG

pointing to me to explain why he was talking to the French man. I then became concerned that maybe it had not been a good idea to tell Uncle Otto, because of possible consequences for this French prisoner of war. Because he soon disappeared, and I was never told where he was sent, I have always worried if I did the right thing, bringing this to the attention of someone who maybe could have been helpful. After that man was gone, we had another French prisoner to help with the farm labor. Ottmar could not possibly do all that needed to be done. After a while, all French prisoners disappeared, and I have never stopped wondering if more harm came to them later than they experienced working in our little village. Our next workers were Baraska and Fritz. They had to do the work that would have been left undone without their help.

* * *

WHILE Uncle Otto and Tante Lizzy were in Hausa, my two uncles must have decided when I would best be moved to Aschaffenburg. Perhaps it was during this visit that Uncle Otto walked with me to Trennfeld to show me where I needed to go in order to get to the train station there. During their visits, Otto and Lizzy occupied the best room in the house. It was upstairs and had a beautiful ceiling with a three-dimensional circular design, and the colors red, blue, and gold. The room had windows facing east as well as south. That gave them a view of the Linden Tree I was so fond of. I always thought of the history that that tree might have witnessed. It had a red sandstone wall around its roots and a red sandstone bench around its huge trunk. Town meetings were held under it and a small water fountain was at its side, where one could pump water for drinking or for flowers. That is the very place Helena Baunach called me a foreigner many years ago, just before I started kindergarten.

HOW I LEARNED I WAS A FOREIGNER

I thought that Papa Ottmar was my father, just as I thought that Mama Karolina was my mother. I thought that until I was called names by a girl named Helena. She was much older than me, at least it seemed like it at the time, and this event took place under the Linden Tree. This tree was a mighty tree in the middle of Hausa. People stopped and chatted there. It was the center of the village.

It was under this tree, by the fountain, that I stood. I do not recall why I was there, but I am sure Mama Karolina had encouraged me to go out and be with the other children. This is one of my earliest memories. For whatever reason, Helena, standing next to her younger sister, called

Finding Out I am a Foreigner.

over to me that I should go home, as I had no business there since I was
an American.

"*Gea doch henni, du Amerikaner,*" she yelled in the Franconian dialect. I had never heard what an American was and therefore had no idea
what that could mean. But I knew by the tone of her voice that it somehow was not a good thing to be. I said I was no such thing, and I was
shocked that someone would be angry at me for any reason. I wanted to
stay there among the other children. After all, Mama Karolina had sent
me there to mix with others. She must have thought that, at four years of
age, I should start to be on my own some of the time. Helena, however,
was determined to make me miserable and screamed some more at me.
I started to cry and ran towards home.

When I got there, Mama Karolina was surprised to see me after such
a short time, and that I was crying, and she asked me what was wrong.
I repeated what Helena had called me. Karolina explained to me that
Helena had not been very nice to yell at me, but that in fact I was an
Amerikaner, yet that was not a bad thing to be. She said that America
is another country and that I had been born there, and was sent there
to Hausa to grow up. Well, I did not like to be different than the other
children, and was not really happy to hear this. I wondered how I was
going to fit in without being called names. Mama said I might like to be
glad that I was an American.

At that moment, that was just a bit much to absorb, in addition to
realizing that Mama Karolina was not my real mother. Gradually, I must
have asked more questions that helped me understand the situation. And
Mama Karolina promised to talk to Helena, to tell her that she should
not call me names. And that was really helpful. Mama Karolina also
showed me the fur coat that my mother had sent her. I was also shown
letters from my father and mother, and near Christmastime, packages
from them would arrive with sugar and coffee and chocolate, because,
by then, things like that were becoming difficult to get in Germany.

GASTHAUS ZUM GRÜNEN BAUM

Gasthaus z. gr. Baum

P APA Ottmar was the youngest of five brothers born to Apolonia and
Phillip in Hausa. Because the small fields could not be divided into
five portions, plans were made to send four of the brothers elsewhere,
and to give most of the land to Ottmar. Heinrich did get some land, and
he also married a local woman with some fields and stayed in the village. Karl Alfons, my father, also inherited some land, but he became a
butcher and emigrated to the United States after a a stint in the German
army during the first World War. His brother Gustave had died in that
war. Meanwhile, Otto was educated and became a language teacher.

Ottmar was a short, heavy man, cleanly shaven most of the time. He
married Karolina Luder and produced no offspring. He and Karolina
managed not only the farming, but also the bar. In a wirtschaft, the lack

of a bar counter encourages conversation and makes the place a social environment for members of the local community. Many opinions were presented here, and often consensus was reached, through talks during this period. So a wirtschaft was not only a place to drink beer and relax, but also a place where village business was agreed upon. Not only local events but national and international events were discussed there, and people voiced their opinions and beliefs about those events. Also, sometimes agreements were never reached and factions were formed there.

The name of this particular wirtschaft was and still is *Gasthaus zum Grünen Baum*. Translated, this means "Guesthouse of the Leafy Tree." As in most German establishments of this kind, as well as some other businesses, there hung a sign above the door indicating it was a public place for people to come in and have a drink or purchase something. This sign was a green circle of leaves around a star. For all one could see, it was a Star of David. In this case, it did not claim that the place was Jewish; rather, this star came from alchemy, indicating brewing activity. I know the sign well because I repainted it several times in my life.

This is Mama Karolina and Uncle Ottmar on the other side of the Gasthaus

View of the Gasthaus from the Courtyard.

Uncle Ottmar, me, and Mama Karolina

Me on my rocking horse.

Weihnachten is the biggest holiday in Germany. In English it translates to "Holy Night" and means Christmas. It is both a Catholic holiday and a family holiday. Hausa was a Catholic village and one was expected to attend midnight mass. Families with small children might find some relative to stay home with the kids. It was not a sin to not attend. It was just expected that anyone who could go, would do so.

Since everyone knew everyone in the village, everyone knew who was there and who was not. There were about 300 to 350 inhabitants in Hausa. Everyone was a peasant farmer. No one really had any secrets to keep.

The Christmas season opened with Advent. This started four weeks before Weihnachten. Many families, as well as the church, had advent wreaths hanging from a ceiling. These had four candles, often red. Each week, another candle was lit. This custom was more popular in cities than in villages. Farmers just did not have the time for it.

December 6th is St. Nicholas's holiday. He is the patron saint of children. In the cities, one would see some adult males dressed as bishops. I remember seeing that in Aschaffenburg when I lived with Uncle Otto and Tante Lizzy. Tante Lizzy had an advent wreath, but she never had a man dressed as a bishop come to Herrlein Strasse #3. She did give me an advent calendar with little cardboard windows I could open and close. I was glad to have one of those. They were shiny and had illustrations of angels, winter scenes, shepherds, wise men, and anything related to the season. I'm sure I was too impatient to wait for the actual dates to open the windows, and opened them all at once, and then closed them to open them again as the actual calendar days came.

Another item I associate with Weihnachten is the *Lebkuchen*. These were a type of ginger cookie. Most often they came in the shape of hearts, with a ribbon, so you could hang them around your neck. There usually was hard icing forming designs or even words, depending on the holiday. At Christmastime they were often smaller and came in decorative containers. They were also softer and had chocolate coverings or had nuts in them. Nürnberg was and still is the capital of gingerbread cookies.

Springerle is another type of cookie. The dough is special, and the cookies usually have a design on them. This design can be made with a rolling pin that has designs carved into it or with metal pieces that you can press into the dough. The cookies have to be floured so they won't stick. And they have to be allowed to dry overnight to keep the design. These were my favorite because they were crisp and had anise in them. The word "Springerle" might refer to a jumping or running horse and comes from the pre-Christian tradition of offering live animals to the gods. Poorer people baked animal-shaped things and offered those to the gods.

Now I need to tell you about St. Nicholas Day. In Hausa, two young men dressed up, or perhaps down, into old clothes, with long coats and ropes or chains about their waists. They were noisy in coming into the living quarters of the house. Their faces were obscured so you could not know who they were. Often, hemp ropes were taken apart into their individual fibers, and these became the hair or beards of these ruffians. Their eyes were mostly hidden, which served to make them more scary.

They also had hemp sacks, which were usually used as potato bags by the farmers. Any child could imagine being stuffed into one of these bags. I am sure my first reaction, when I first experienced this, was fear of being taken away, and utter surprise that Uncle Ottmar and Mama Karolina would allow such goings-on in their house. Yes, they had informed me that Knecht Ruprecht (St. Nicholas's companion) would come to the house, and I should not be afraid, for I would get some nuts and apples, which was the reason they had sacks. In spite of these reassurances, I clung tightly to Mama Karolina's skirt, behind which I tried to hide myself. I also formed the opinion that I could very well live without Knecht Ruprecht ever coming again. Of course, this happened every year.

Later in life, I discovered—from readings—where this tradition came from. It came from pre-Christian belief in the German gods of Valhalla. There, the primary god was Wotan. It was said that Wotan would descend from the beauty of Valhalla in order to check on his subjects, human beings, to see if they treated each other with kindness. In order not to be recognized when he met them, he dressed as an old man. If he was treated well, he knew his subjects were kind to each other. That was the reason for the kind of clothes Knecht Ruprecht came dressed in. These men at the house were boisterous just because they were young and could not imagine otherwise; and, of course, it was tradition.

When I was thirteen, a mother in Hausa who was not comfortable with this tradition asked me if I would come to her boys dressed as a bishop on St. Nicholas Day. I was only too happy to oblige, and got busy creating a cardboard miter for my head. Mama Karolina helped me with something to wear that could be interpreted as a bishop's dress. The problem was creating a curved staff. I avoided that by simply creating a cross on top of a broomstick. I had no one else to come with me, so I went alone.

This family's house had an enormous red sandstone staircase, and in the dark of night, I had a hard time getting up it as there was no railing.

I don't think I was a total success as the bishop, but was glad that two boys did not have to endure the fear and noise of Knecht Ruprecht. That house, on a dead end street, has since been knocked down.

One other thing that one could state about Christmas in Germany at the time, and particularly in villages, is that there were no outdoor decorations. The Christmas tree was really the only decorated item in the house. Often, the tree to be used might have been decided upon way in advance, in the spring of the year. The reason for that was that, at that time of the year, it was necessary to replenish the pile of wood each family had been using all winter long for cooking and heating. Each peasant farmer had at least one woodlot that served him wood. All cooking was done on kitchen stoves using split wood from trees that had to be cut down in the woodlot. It required these to be sawed into small enough lengths to be able to fit within the openings of the stove. This generally required two people to use a large saw with a wooden handle on either end, to saw back and forth until each piece fell off the tree trunk. These pieces then had to be split. This could be done at the site or at home, depending on the weather and the individual farmer's circumstances. In our case, the rounds were loaded onto a wagon and brought by horse to the north side of the barn. There, they lay in wild profusion until time allowed the splitting to be done. Yet one could not wait too long because the splitting became more difficult over time, and, in addition, you had to stack them so that the wood could dry over the summer, so it could burn well in the winter.

So while one was occupied with felling a tree, one might spot a fir tree just the right size to fit into the particular place in the house designated for it on Christmas. One might purposefully choose an imperfect tree that could be made to look better by drilling extra holes where branches could be added. The more perfect trees could then be left to grow up to be sold for timber.

The smaller branches were gathered into bundles that were later used to start the fires. This work was mostly done by the women and children, so the men did the job of sawing, loading, and splitting. Some farmers did not have enough room at home to store all their wood. These farmers had to leave the stacked wood near the edge of the forest where the trees had been felled. Then they had to get portions of this supply to bring home, all through the winter.

We were lucky to have enough room in a woodshed, or even just outside the shed. We, having two guest rooms that had to be heated, needed a great deal of ready wood all winter. This shed also housed an apple press that allowed Ottmar to make his own cider. Part of the cider was consumed as sweet cider, but most of it was allowed to turn into hard cider that could be served to guests plain or mixed with seltzer water. The latter was called a *Shorle*. You could also order a wine shorle. The hard cider was called *Most*. It was also the base for a Christmas drink called *Glüwein*. That involved heating the most with cinnamon and honey and other spices, and was reserved for the Christmas season.

Since I was small, one of my jobs was to enter through the tiny doors of the cider barrels to clean its insides. My shoes had to be very clean before I was allowed to squeeze myself into these barrels. I could not stand up straight inside. It was awkward work, using stiff brushes to scrub the inside. It probably needed the use of vinegar as a final cleaning. Cloths and sponges had to be handed out through the barrel for rinsing. When it all was done to the best of my ability, I was allowed out and then a cardboard strip infused with sulfur was lit and hung up inside the barrel with the lid on. This sulfur theoretically killed any live bacteria still inside the barrel. If the most turned out well, one knew the cleaning job had been done well. This part of Christmas had to be done in apple season.

The apple press was an enormous round piece of red sandstone, perhaps twenty inches from the floor. It had a trough about three inches deep that cut all the way around the flat top. In the center was a thick, metal pole with swivels cut into it so it could be turned down tightly onto the squashed apples. There were also four huge sections that were held in place to hold the mass of crushed apples. When the proper wheels were turned, the liquid rushed out into deep wooden containers. This process produced sweet apple cider, which was only drinkable for a few days. It had to be brought to the ready barrels in the wine cellar. And this, for whatever strange reason, was not in any part of the cellar beneath our house, but under the cow barn of the neighbor across the street. But that cellar belonged to us.

There were steep red sandstone steps that led down into this arched stone cellar, where the temperature was equally cool the entire year. This was perfect for the sweet cider to turn into hard cider. Some of the hard apple cider could also be turned into apple wine through a second process. This required that the liquid be put into other newly cleaned barrels. The hard cider was transferred via a rubber tube that you had to suck the air out of first. Only Uncle Ottmar knew how to do this. This wine was a specialty of the Zum Grünen Baum.

Now that we have gotten to hard cider and glüwein and past Knecht Ruprecht, I still need to discuss how Christmas Eve was celebrated. *Christkindl* arrived on Christmas Eve or Christmas Day in the evening. For this, teenage girls got dressed up in pairs. Perhaps two sisters or two friends of slightly different ages would conspire to come to houses of families that had requested them to come. These two also did not bring any presents; the presents you got were from your parents; this was clear to everyone. I remember one particular Christmas because there were two sisters who came to the house, and I immediately saw through their disguises. It was Helena Baunach and her younger sister, Anna. It was Helena who had called me names and had me running, crying, into the arms of Mama Karolina.

The younger Anna was dressed in white, in what was most likely her Holy Communion dress. Her hair was combed down in front of her face so I could not see it, and she was in front of her taller sister, Helena, who also had dark hair combed down over her face. Helena had dark clothes on. She was representing Hullafra, and Anna was representing

Chriskindl, the Christ child. They announced themselves with a little bell in the space between the outer house door and the door to the room we were in. This room was the smaller of the two guest rooms we had, and we used it as our Christmas room because it was nicely connected to the kitchen. Also, there was a stove in it that could heat the space, and wood for the stove was in the kitchen. In addition, the room was big enough for the Christmas tree on one end, and had plenty of sitting room for the family and guests.

After Christkindl had managed to give me the cookies Mama Karolina had left in the space between the two doors, they both left. I think I mostly felt embarrassment for the two girls, who were trying their best. The *Hullafra* was from pre-Christian origin and represented Hulda, the wife of Wotan. In a practical sense, it was her job to get Christkindl safely from one place to another.

So now we had cookies and *glüwein* and presents on the table under the tree. The tree itself had ornaments that came out of the cardboard boxes where they had been kept for years. My favorite ornaments were the silver glass birds with little white glass feathers that came out of their bodies in the rear. There were also round ornaments that had indentations on the front that multiplied the reflections of the lights of the room and the wax candles that were fastened to the branches of the tree with tiny metal clips. How and where these tiny candles were clipped was of utmost importance to prevent any fires from occurring. It was also essential that once they were lit, the tree could never be left alone, not for even a moment. In addition, the tree had to be moved from this guest room that very evening if the next day the Wirtschaft was open to the public. In that case, the tree had to be carried out the door, across the hall, into the private family/office room. That meant, of course, that the tree had to be light enough and small enough to carry and fit through these doors.

In some other homes where the tree did not have to be moved, those families could opt for a larger tree. But it seemed to me that most people had their tree on a table. I suspect the trees were not kept very long as they would dry out and be more prone to fire with the live candles on them.

The best part of Weihnachten was the many wonderful Christmas songs that everyone knew. One could visit other homes and sing with members of those families. I loved the places that had a crèche (nativity scene). Our family never seemed to get that together. We did, one winter, get a rather fancy play farm with lambs and cows. I used that as a sort of crèche without any baby Jesus, and I did get a fabulous rocking horse once. That came from Nazi friends of Uncle Ottmar, as far as I could tell.

This brings me to the end of my memories of Weihnachten in Germany

Winter Scene (acrylic)

Meeting Baraska and Mitro.

ONE summer day, in about 1940, at the age of eight, I was out by the woodshed when someone called me urgently at the top of their lungs to come to the *Wirtsstube*. This was the main guest room that seated the most people at the Gasthaus zum Grünen Baum. I dropped whatever I was doing and ran past the rear of the stable to the door to the narrow corridor that connected the north side of the property to the main yard, where the rear door of this room was located.

I had expected to be given some task that had to be performed immediately, or perhaps to be chided because I had not done something I was supposed to have done earlier. But neither was the case; I was totally surprised. Instead, there were several people standing, watching and waiting for me to come through the door. What could that mean?

Uncle Ottmar was standing near the bar, his hands crossed over his chest, looking important. Slightly to his left, near one of the two pillars on either side of the heating stove—now cold because it was high summer—was a stranger. I took a few steps into the room and turned left to see two new figures seated on the bench right next to the door I had just come in. I turned more fully to see them. Uncle Ottmar said, "This is Baraska and her husband." He must have said the husband's name but I was busy trying to understand the first new name. What kind of name was that? "Baraska." I had never heard of such a name! It was foreign to my ears. (Recently I learned his name was "Mitro.")

Here was this couple with foreign sounding names, and both of them barefoot. That was very unusual. No one in Hausa walked around barefoot. Concerned about their feet, I looked more closely to see if they were injured, but they seemed to be in perfect condition. In fact, the feet looked as if they always walked about barefoot and were used to that. And I noticed the strong contrast between the bare feet and the dress Baraska had on.

Baraska had on what I thought was a linen dress. I had seen linen bed sheets in dresser drawers and knew their look was different from that of cotton sheets. Linen seemed coarser, but stronger than cotton. The color of her dress was also a natural color, not bleached white. I would call it ecru. And it looked new. Not only did it look new, it was also embroidered in cross-stitch in black and red in many places, especially around the borders. I later learned this style was typical in the Ukraine. It was perfectly done. It was truly beautiful. It was definitely not meant for everyday wear. My mind jumped to the word *die braut* (bride). This was reinforced by the fact that her husband, whose name I never learned, had on black pants and a white shirt with a black vest. I thought he must be the groom.

"Oh my gosh!" I thought. "These people were taken just as they came out of the church where they were married." And here they were, in a strange and possibly evil place that they had been transported to, possibly against their will.

The two of them stared silently straight ahead or down at the floor. They looked captive, and were, and could do nothing about it. I was not sure how I felt, but I was impressed by their stoicism, finding themselves in this place, home to me but strange to them. Ottmar then told me that Baraska would be working in our house, and that her husband would be working in another household. And he mentioned the household, but it did not register until he mentioned one of the children, Elwira, who lived there. Elwira's father, like so many other men, was in the military, and Elwira, her sister, and their mother could not possibly do all the farming work that had to be done in order to secure them a livelihood for that year and the next. After all was clear to me, Uncle Ottmar motioned to the man who had brought Baraska and her husband that we needed to go on to the next step.

Visiting Baraska and Hearing Nazi Propaganda.

At first I did not know where Baraska and her husband were quartered. I only found out later, when she was ready to deliver her first child, a daughter. No one had lived in the house where they stayed for several years. The previous owners were old, and either they were childless, or their children must have been able to build a new home for themselves. It was a typical house of the area. Like all houses of Franconia it was half-timbered. Between the heavy timbers were branches cut to just fit about a foot apart. Straw had been woven through the branches and mud had been applied. Over that was a coat of stucco which preserved and weather-proofed all that was beneath. The roofs were made of baked red tiles. Older homes often had coats of moss in their tiles, depending on the amount of light they received.

Baraska had been working, mostly in the fields, until the day she birthed her daughter. And her working in the fields gave Karolina more time for housework. Still, Karolina had to go out in the fields when there was an urgency to complete some work because of an impending change in the weather. Anyone familiar with farm work understands that rain at the wrong time can be disastrous to the harvest of grains and hay. And wet hay leads to rot and potentially to fire if it gets too hot in the process of fermenting.

Baraska was really very much needed in the household, and she worked hard, as everyone did. I remember on one occasion, Fritz, Baraska, and I were required to go to a far-away field, west of the village, to get fodder for the cows and pigs. In this instance, it meant gathering the outer leaves of a type of beet called *Runkel*. This meant kneeling or crouching low to the ground for several hours in order to get enough for all the animals. First you had to strip the dried leaves off the beet. These were left to rot on the soil. Then you had to remove some of the next layer of leaves. These were laid on a string. When enough had been placed, with about half of the leaf tips pointing one way and the remainder pointing the other way, one had to close the string tight enough that you could lift the bundle with one hand, but not so tight that you crushed the stems of the leaves. These bundles were either placed on a wagon or a wheelbarrow to bring back to the barnyard.

You can see that this was very hard and very boring work for anyone. Well, for me, it was dreadful, and I made no bones about it. I was not a good worker but rather a liability to both Fritz and Baraska. My boredom led me to bother Baraska. A few times I got up from my crouching position and ran to Baraska to tug at her kerchief or to pull the collar of her blouse. This was nothing terrible, but clearly annoying to someone who was forced to do this boring and hard work. Fritz let it go just two times before he started to scream at me to leave Baraska alone. Both of them were really slaves on that farm. I, on the other hand, was a member of the family. I was glad that Fritz asserted himself and stopped me from bothering Baraska while she was doing her best to get the work done.

The other benefit of stripping the leaves was that it was good for the plant. It stopped the plant from spending energy on growing the leaves

Me Teasing Baraska.

that were removed, so that it could spend energy on the beet. The leaves were a very important pig fodder and were put in silos at some point to be fed to the pigs and other animals in the winter months.

Since we had no animals with us to bring the load to the barnyard, we left the bundles at the edge of the field to be picked up the next day, and we brought back just a few on a wheelbarrow for that evening's fodder.

In the winter, on Sundays, when Baraska was not working or was working only enough to feed the animals, I was sent to the very old house she and her husband lived in in order to bring them food. This entire house was without heat, as were most houses in the village. But there was a large heating stove in one room around which the bed and their few belongings were placed. Together, they brought two girls into the world. Much later, after the war had stopped and Germany was defeated, the Russians came and took Baraska and her husband—and all the other Polish people who worked in the village—away.

Although this village, and the whole area, was in the American sector after the war, the Russians were permitted to come in to repatriate those who had been taken out of their sphere of interest. The Russian officers had a meal at Gasthaus zum Grünen Baum. They wanted something to eat while Baraska and her husband were busy loading the truck with their possessions. By the time they had finished eating, the truck was loaded and I found Baraska standing on it with all the stuff she was taking with her. Her hands were at her side, and she was crying desperately. I felt so sorry for her. Here she was being commandeered again by people of another nation, with them telling her what she must do. And I am sure she did not know with certainty where she was going. To think that she had spent all that time of her life working in fields that were not her own and now she was being taken away from what she knew again without any guarantees about her future. To me, it was heartbreaking, and I will never forget that terrible feeling.

Baraska came down and embraced Mama Karolina, and soon, the

motor started and the wheels turned. We waved, and off they went. We had no idea where they were headed either. It must have been nearly as terrible to her as the time she had been commandeered by the Germans to leave her home village. Such is war. Such is the lack of human kindness.

Baraska Leaves.

10

FRITZ KONRAD

...itz, Mama Carolina, me, and Uncle Ottmar.

O NE day of indifferent weather and of no remembered quality, there was Fritz, awkwardly turning his cap around in his hands, not sure where to look or whom to notice. He was standing in the restaurant part of the house. Uncle Ottmar said to no one in particular that Fritz would now be staying with us. He would be housed here and would work here. Fritz grinned, unsure of what else to do. I felt sorry for him. I imagined being brought into a strange house. Yet I was also glad that I would no longer be the only minor in the house. I had, at times, wondered why I had no brothers or sisters, as some of the other children had.

I had been asked to fetch wood or coal for the stoves, but I had not been asked to plow or load the wagons with manure, as some other youngsters had started to do, even though I was their age. I was aware that I had not gone to the first grade with the others my age, but had been held back. That was because I was smaller, and therefore weaker.

Fritz, on the other hand, was sturdy compared to me, and probably older than me. Uncle Ottmar soon announced that we would eat and that Fritz would use the bedroom across the hall from me. And so it was for a while. But that did not last too long. Before long, we had a Polish man who slept in the small room across the hall, and Fritz was moved into my room, which was big and was in the front of the house, facing the street and the restaurant sign, hung just outside one of the windows. I was glad that I had a roommate. Later, this became a problem for everyone.

It may have been in the winter, when the unheated room was just very uncomfortable to get undressed in—as was getting into a cold bed— that it occurred to me that Fritz would be a warm body next to which I would feel warmer, and no sooner had I thought that than I asked if I could go to his bed. Fritz did not seem against it, and I hopped across the room and slid into the warmth that was Fritz.

I was amazed at how much bigger Fritz was than me and I snuggled close. I explored his body and soon found an erection. This was something new to me, and I wondered if I were to grow one at some point. But in the meantime, Fritz's erection would do.

At some point, he persuaded me to go to my bed, and I only went after he promised me that I could get in bed with him at another time. And indeed it became common and this led to jerking off. And since there were no tissues or toilet paper or anything other than old newspapers, this became a problem, and the only thing to do was to ejaculate on the wooden floor. That became a problem when Mina, who came to live there, complained that we had spat on the floor. Fritz and I looked at each other then and could barely keep ourselves from bursting out with laughter.

At another time, Fritz made us go into the urinal across the hall. This was primitive. It was just a wall painted a shiny black color, along which there was a cement trough that ran into a hole that had a metal plate on it with holes, so that urine could flow into the sewage pit that was under part of the yard, and the manure pile. And the only reason that such a thing existed was because, before the war got into full swing, the Gasthaus zum Grünen Baum had dances in the Tanz Saal. And of course, since that was a public event, there had to be a bathroom for the men. The women had to go downstairs. Now that the war was going on, and all the men were at war and there was austerity, who would even consider holding a dance? The dance hall was now basically a storage room. And it is still so after all these years. If people want to dance now, the village has built a new building just for that.

But back to Fritz and me. Whenever I was in the village and Fritz was willing, we would value our togetherness. However, since this was a Catholic village and I had to go to confession in order to eventually take Holy Communion, I was aware that what Fritz and I were up to was a sin, and that I would have to confess it to the priest. I had learned that what I told the priest was a secret between me and the priest, or perhaps God. And also Fritz would have to confess it whether he ever had Holy Communion or not.

Well, this secret must have had a leak. Because not too long after confession, and now that it was warmer, Fritz was moved to the dance hall. Well this did not sit well with me. I wanted to be with Fritz and not stay alone in my bedroom, so I traipsed all the way to the dance hall and slipped in with Fritz.

I had one of the very big books we had, ready near the bed, and as soon as anyone was heard coming up the stairs, and ever so nicely asked how we were doing, the book was hauled onto the bed and we, I in particular, showed Mama Karolina that we were engrossed in the reading about the First World War, in which my uncle Gustave had fallen. And there were so many pictures to prove how well the German men had fought in that war! I smiled convincingly at Mama. Perhaps she did not want to create a fuss, and she moved on, asking me again to go back to my bed as soon as we were done looking at the book. Fritz, of course, was not a child of the family. His position was more tenuous than mine, so he encouraged me to get back to my room and then really pleaded with me. I had to agree that he did have a reason to worry, and I eventually did go to my lonely bedroom.

This was not the last of our get-togethers, but Fritz made it clear a little at a time that I was invading his privacy, and he eventually fended me off. But looking back on this, I realize that, even at an early age, I knew where my leanings would be for the rest of my life.

I also learned a lot about social positions and that what some people can allow themselves, others cannot. Fritz's social position was made clear in many ways. He was expected to feed the animals; gather maize, which he had to shred with an electric machine; lift heavy things; and get dirty. I helped many times, and my job was to clean out the pig sties, and I was proud that I could do a good job of that. But I knew that when I resided in Aschaffenburg during the school year, it fell on Fritz's shoulders to do that as well. He earned his keep over and over on a daily basis.

Even on those days when I arrived or left by train, he had to walk with a child's wagon all the way to the train station two villages away to get me and my suitcase, so that I would not have to carry it all that distance. I will never forget the long walks from and to the train. On one occasion, Fritz pointed to a figure standing by a glass-less window in a barn quite far away, and said that that person was his sister. I had not known that he had a sister, and I could not imagine how he knew it was her from so far away. I suggested that we go nearer, so he could talk with her. But he shook his head. His family was so long ago for him, and he was not going to be able to go back to something he had left behind, and which would give him grief. I never found out just what did happen to his parents and how he was taken from them. I have since read that, during National Socialist times under Hitler, many families that were not considered well-functioning were simply split up, and the children were given to a family that was thought to be better suited to raise children. In Fritz's case, he was given to Uncle Ottmar, who was a party member and indeed was *Burgomeister* (Mayor) of Holzkirchhausen for several years, and who needed a worker. Fritz's parents may have been institutionalized, or, for all we know, they may have been sent to concentration camps.

Fritz worked many more years under Uncle Ottmar. Some years after I had moved to the United States, I came back to the village and asked where he was. I was told he had gotten a job in one of the western cities in the Ruhrgebiet. I never did find out where exactly, but he did come to visit on his motorbike when he had free time. He supposedly had a girlfriend. That was nice to hear, but I felt sorry that he was not really given anything in return for all his labor. And the last thing I heard was that he had died in an accident on one of his trips back to the village. I always shrink a little inside when I think of this.

Gentleman with Tie (pencil and ink)

11

MY MOVE TO ASCHAFFENBURG

Mama Karolina and me in Ashaffenburg.

WHILE I was living in Hausa, I attended kindergarten and was there for two years. I was kept back for a year because I was so small that people thought I should mature for another year before going on to first grade.

Kindergarten was relatively new then and had been introduced by the National Socialists. The person in charge was from another part of Germany, and the assistant was Rösla, from the family that operated the post office. A lot of families did some type of work, in addition to farming, that needed to be done in the village. For example, one family would be butchers and another woodworkers. Woodworking included building coffins, with special tools and skills, and any other type of carpentry that was required in the village. There were also two tiny stores that sold sugar, spices, rice, and farina—items one could use in the kitchen.

I was lucky that the kindergarten was just a garden or two away from our house. One could wave from one window to the other. That made it easy for Karolina and me.

Around that time, when I was five- or six-years old, Ottmar and my uncle Otto in Aschaffenburg must have had talks about my future. There also might have been letters from my parents. I was six-years old in 1938. The Depression was basically over in the United States, and perhaps life was better for my parents. I recall that my mother sometimes sent pack-

This plate depicts the Schloss Johannisburg (Johannisburg Castle) in Aschaffenburg.

ages which included coffee and chocolate. These were highly welcomed. Coffee was becoming hard to get, and chocolate was also a luxury! One package had a beautiful fake fur coat for Karolina. No one else in the village had ever seen such a fine coat. Karolina seldom wore it, partly because it made her stand out next to the other women.

Since I was likely to go back to my parents in Brooklyn, it made sense to have me grow up in a city instead of in Hausa, the tiny village of 300 people. So plans were made that, at some point, I would live at least part-time in Aschaffenburg. Not only would that prepare me for city life, but it would also spread the responsibility of my upbringing over the two brothers, Ottmar and Otto, and their wives. Karolina and Ottmar had no children and neither did Otto and Lizzy. Lizzy, however, had in fact born three boys, but they had each died early in childhood. This made it a very different thing for Lizzy to take me in as opposed to Karolina, who had had no births. Lizzy agreed to take me in, so plans were made for me to attend school in Aschaffenburg.

My move required that I learn how to travel from Hausa to Aschaffenburg by walking all the way from the village to the nearest train station, in Trennfeld. Trennfeld was quite some distance away. We had to walk over the mountain to the north to get to Wüstenzell. After we had gotten to the main street down in the valley, we climbed the second mountain, going northwest. This mountain was less steep but longer. Thank goodness the weather held and the harvested grain fields allowed us to see ahead. If the wheat had still been standing, we could not have seen where the turn was and could have gotten lost. We might have missed the path that allowed us to go along the edge of Homburg. At some point slightly north of Homburg, there was a ferry, across the Main, to Trennfeld. And it was another kilometer from the ferry to the train station. This had to be learned. Eventually it fell on Uncle Otto to walk the route with me. Once I had learned this, I would have to walk it on my own. As it happened, Fritz was from Trennfeld, and he walked the route with me many times. During those years I spent school months in Aschaffenburg and vacation times in Hausa.

While I was still in school in Hausa, we learned the Roman letters by working with a package of letters that one could place into words on a board that came in a kit. In the winter, we had to bring pieces of wood to heat the room. There was a wood- and coal-fired stove in the room. In school, we spoke High German, and on the playground and elsewhere, we spoke the local dialect. We heard High German on the radio and the songs and prayers in Church were in High German, as well. No one was confused about which was which. And yet, much later, the Bavarian government forbade parents to speak the dialect with their children, and now the dialect, I believe, has ceased to exist.

It must have been in 1941, when I was nine years old, that Uncle Otto walked with me to Trennfeld's train station. He wanted to show me Homburg on the way as it had a medieval tower standing by itself in the town square. It had been converted into a home for a family. He also wanted me to know that this village was famous for its wines. All the sun made the grapes as sweet as they could get in Germany. And the ground was calciferous and stony. This gave the wine its prized taste. This was *Frankenwein*, and Uncle Otto wanted me to know that.

"Karlchen," he said at one point. "This wine is never exported. This wine, the Germans keep to themselves. We export the Mosel wine and the Rhine wine but not the Main wine." After this lesson was a stop in a wine shop, where I was allowed to taste the wine.

Earlier, while Uncle Otto was busy looking over the wall at the river, I saw a boy come out of a house. He was dressed differently than most boys, in that he had long pants on. And they were striped in white and blue. He also had curls over his ears. He started to throw stones at me. I had been told that in Homburg there lived Jewish families, and I assumed that this boy was Jewish. He did not actually hurt me, but on the other hand, I had never had anyone throw stones at me before. So I was afraid and walked over to Uncle Otto for safety.

In winter, German boys wore stockings that reached way past the knees, under our short pants. The stockings were held in place with rubber bands. I remember that vividly because when stockings were hard to get, Tante Lizzy got me a pair that were sheer torture to put on. They scratched so terribly it was just unbelievable. And I had to put them on no matter what. Things got more scarce as the war went on.

After the wine shop, we stumbled down the steep street to the main road, following the river. This street was so steep it was almost a staircase. It had red sandstone stones embedded in its surface, across its width, so it looked like steps. At the bottom, we reached the main highway past the cement factory, between the road and the river. After a kilometer or so, we came to the ferry that allowed us to cross the river for a small fee. The ferry was attached to a rope so it would not be washed down the river, which was flowing in a southerly direction at that point.

Once in Trennfeld, one could get a local train that traveled south to Wertheim. Uncle Otto showed me how to buy the train ticket, and that I had to specify *Süd Bahnhof*, which meant the south train station, as opposed to *Haupt Bahnhof*, which was the main and larger station. After I embarked on the train, it was fun to see the village flash by, and the river was mostly in view. When we got to Wertheim, we turned west, into a narrow valley. There were quite a few stops in villages on this route before Süd Bahnhof. From there, it was a kilometer walk to Otto and Lizzy's house. The villages on this route were not harmed in the war. And neither were the train tracks between them, because they were not part of the faster track system that was moving military goods and weapons.

When Fritz came with me to Trennfeld, we avoided Homburg altogether. We just walked past that village on its back side. It actually shortened the trip by half a kilometer. The area was very beautiful because it had calcium-sided mountains facing due west, which allowed it to receive a lot of sunlight. On the west side of the river was the Spessart, which was a heavily-wooded and mountainous area. Aschaffenburg lay on the far west side of the Spessart. The train from Trennfeld followed the Main south, to Wertheim. There, the river and train turned west, toward Miltenberg, and then north, to get to Aschaffenburg. From there, the river flowed west to Frankfurt and then to Mainz, where it emptied into the Rhine River. These small river cities were spared any bombings. They have all the old houses from centuries ago, and are models of middle-age architecture even today.

Fritz and I walked that distance many times. He, of course, had to walk back to Hausa on his own. I would have a suitcase for which we used a little wagon to carry, and then he would bring the wagon back to the village, to the family from which we had borrowed it. We had some liquid and some sandwiches for this long walk.

I recently called my second cousin Eva in Hausa. She said, "Karl, you have to tell people that this is a twenty-kilometer walk. I guess the reason you could do that is because, at that time, you were used to walking, because all the people, including the children, walked from one farm field to another, and home again for lunch, and in the evening, home again for supper. Then there was the walking from the barn to the stable, back and forth, until all the chores were done."

12

UNCLE OTTO

Uncle Otto.

UNCLE Otto was the only brother who was granted a college education. This was quite rare for the time, in these small villages. Dividing the land would have left the family in poverty. Otto paid for his college education with his portion of the inheritance.

Uncle Otto had elected to become a student of languages. He learned French and English. I think he studied French in or near Pirmasens, close to the French border. I think this because his wife, Elizabeth Grobholz, came from a patrician family in that city. I was informed that Lizzy had a tendency to feel superior to her husband's peasant family. When she and Uncle Otto came to Hausa for a visit, she wanted to have her and Otto's meals served in a different room. She and Otto would dine in one of the restaurant dining rooms, as opposed to the large kitchen where everyone else in the family dined. Her attitude of superiority was very present. I must have learned that at an early age.

Up to this point, Uncle Otto was not involved in many things. He was completely unaware of all that was going on around him. He was often reading the newspaper, or on a long walk in the countryside.

I stayed in the village until I was nine years old. I attended the National Socialist Kindergarten. There was a garden between the villagers' wing and the kindergarten, next door.

After I attended two years of primary school, I started to hear rumors about my being moved to Aschaffenburg, where Uncle Otto and Tante Lizzy lived. When I lived there, I was glad that the school was not far from where we lived, and I was happy to be living in a building that had beautiful parrots and vines painted around the entrance.

During this time, Uncle Otto was busy teaching at the teachers college. I assume he taught French, English, or both. I was never allowed into his study when—I assume—he was working on his lesson plans. He had a beautiful dark

This is me in the town of Homburg.

oak desk in the Herrnzimmer. This was the largest room of the large apartment in which we lived. It was on the second floor of the house. In the rear of the house was a balcony that overlooked a garden. My bedroom also overlooked the garden. There were two beds in my room. That's where Mama Karolina slept if she came for a visit. I know she came at least once, as there are photos to prove it.

On Sundays, Uncle Otto always went to church. Sometimes, Tante Lizzy also went to church, but she was not as regular as Uncle Otto. He liked to be quiet a lot. He took me on long walks. Because of his silence, I sometimes wondered what was going on in his mind. I asked him once how one could tell if the moon was waxing or waning. He told me if one started the letter "a" in the German word *abnehmen* that meant it was waning and if one started the letter "z" in the German word *zunehmen* that meant the moon was waxing.

I also remember that he had short gray hair, was clean shaven, and wore glasses. He was always well dressed, and he carried a walking stick on his walks.

He almost went out of his way to bring me to see what was happening around us. Once, on a rather long walk outside the city, he brought me to a fenced-in barn in the village outskirts beyond Aschaffenburg. There was a family of people huddled in the straw. He told me they were Jews. No other explanation was offered, and I was afraid to ask.

On another walk, he chose a route that we had never taken, but that was also outside the city proper. It was on the other side of the Main, the river which flows north on the western end of the city. There was a wonderful red sandstone bridge from which you could see the beautiful castle, Johannesburg, and the Pompejanum. The Pompejanum, commissioned by King Ludwig I and built in the 1840's, showed how the Romans lived when they ruled the world. Herr Adalbert Hock had painted the make-believe interior garden, and many decorative details inside. One had to wear felt, slip-on shoes in order to enter the building. This was in addition to paying the admission price. On this particular day, we walked far beyond the bridge, but then turned north.

Soon, we came to a huge fenced-in area full of men walking around. Some were playing a ball game. Uncle Otto did not speak to any of them. I did not know what to make of it. The fence told me they were prisoners. They had uniforms that were not German. I understood they were foreign soldiers, but I did not know from which country and did not ask. I do remember it was a beautiful summer day, and the temperature was perfect. I do not know if we had any more long walks after that. If that was the case, it must have been that the war was beginning to close in on us.

Adalbert Hock's painting of Schloss Johannisburg was incorporated into this emergency banknote after World War I (Aschaffenburg 1921).

W HEN I first came to Herrlein Strasse #3 in Aschaffenburg, I was astonished by the beautifully painted entrance. There were parrots of several colors. I remember one in particular that had a lot of bright blue feathers on the back and wings. I had never seen a real parrot, of course, so I had no idea if that was really the way parrots looked, but I believed it to be true. The details were so realistically painted that they left no doubt in my mind as to the authenticity of the birds. There were also leaves and branches on which the birds sat and fluffed their feathers. I had never seen such an entrance on any house, and would never see the likes of one again. My jaw must have dropped as I found no words for the moment. After all, I had just arrived from the tiny hamlet of Hausa, and I was just a nine-year-old third grader. This was going to be the next chapter of my life. Thus far, I had only been in a city once, to have my tonsils out, and that was in Würzburg, where my Mama Karolina had left me at the hospital. And I had cried so terribly when she left because I thought I would be abandoned.

After my Uncle Otto and I entered the heavy oak door and went up the curved staircase, passing the large window that admitted light into the staircase, we arrived at the apartment door. Uncle Otto took out his key and opened the door to a darker hallway from which several doors opened. Tante Lizzy must have been in the small dining room when she came to greet me. I was somewhat afraid of her as she seemed to be reserved, and I did not know how I was going to be treated by her. I had heard stories from my cousin Otto, who had also been with her and had insisted that he be brought back to Hausa because of the way she had treated him. There was the story that she had sprinkled flour on the floor by his bed, so she would know if he had left the bed to go to the bathroom. Why this presented a problem for her, I never discovered. But I did know I would have to watch out not to displease her. She pointed me to the bedroom that was going to be mine. It was next to a bathroom, and it had a large window overlooking the garden. I liked that. My bed was along the wall next to the bathroom and there was a second bed by the window side.

There must have been supper, and I was very tired. I do not recall when I first mentioned the parrots on the wall of the entrance, but I was told that they had been painted by the owner of the house, who was Adalbert Hock, and that the lady who lived downstairs was his daughter, Anna. It may have been a year or more before I actually met the artist. He seemed to be a living myth, living and working in the house without ever being seen. I remember being walked to the Pompejanum, which was an imitation of a Roman house, which might very well have been built in Ancient Roman times. It was situated west of the Johannesburg castle, in a garden setting overlooking the Main. There, as was customary in Roman times, was a painted garden. I had been told that this had been painted by Herr Hock. That meant that Herr Hock was well known in the area, and was a fixture artist of the city of Aschaffenburg. But I still had not laid eyes on him after all this time.

It was only after I had been admitted to the *Gymnasium* and had an art teacher come to my classroom during my first year that an event occurred that somehow made me bold enough to ask if I could speak to Herr Hock. This was about my dissatisfaction with the sparrows that I had attempted to draw as homework for the art teacher. I was sent to Frau Anna first, to see if she had any objection to my visit to Herr Hock. She hesitated, but seemed to be won over by my entreaties, and she allowed me to go up to the third floor and knock on his door. He was a very old-looking gentleman who seemed dwarfed by the huge window that flooded the room with the north light. There were easels and, mostly, a large floor space that dominated the room. I showed him the work that I had done and told him that I thought the sparrows did not seem to be sitting on the wire the way I thought they should. Herr Hock took a pencil and, on a piece of white paper, made a few scribbly lines, and there appeared three sparrows sitting ever so secure on a thick telephone wire. It was magic, I thought. How could I not have done it just as easily? If Herr Hock could do it, surely I must be able to do so, too. That moment stayed with me all my life. Whether it was consciously or unconsciously, I am not sure, but it did have an impact on me. I was never given another moment with Herr Hock, as far as I can remember, but now I had a real, live person in my memory instead of a myth, and that made a big difference to me. I now knew who had painted those marvelous parrots at the front entrance that I got to see every day. I remember saying to myself, "I want to remember this."

The painting was still by that front door in 2014 when I brought a friend. I wanted him to see the building that I was in when I was bombed during the Second World War. I could see just enough past the wooden slats of the fence to see areas of green leaves and a glimmer of color. Then I went to the middle of the street and put my foot where the bomb had made a crater, and I was glad that, at that time, bombs did not make larger craters, as they do now. It was for this reason, and the fact that it was not a direct hit to the house, that I survived the night when I heard that bomb coming down on us like it was a giant truck, rumbling from above. I made a woodcut of that event when I was taking a workshop at Women's Studio Workshop (see Chapter 16).

14

THE DAY OF THE TRAIN

W HEN I was about nine years old, in 1941, I was sent from the tiny village of Hausa to the city of Aschaffenburg. I was to attend the Gymnasium there and live with my uncle Otto. I was sent to Aschaffenburg a couple of years before I was to attend the Gymnasium, in order for me to get used to living in a city. This meant that I would attend the nearest Volkschule (elementary school). There, we had one teacher for all subjects, unlike in the Gymnasium, where each subject was taught by a different instructor. There were only boys. I had no idea where girls went to school.

In addition to doing regular school work, all students were asked and required to help with the war effort. For elementary students, that meant bringing in bones, for example, or one could pick certain plants that could be made into teas for the soldiers. Some boys had no trouble bringing in bones. I did not care very much for bringing bones and besides, we did not have many of those. I did not quite understand the reason for bringing them. I think they were meant for making soaps. I preferred to pick the assigned plants. Depending on the season and where you lived, you could choose to get raspberry leaves, linden tree blossoms, and *Schachtelkraut*, which I believe is called "horsetail" in English. I had already learned about these in Hausa, where people also made herbal teas.

While it was summer and a beautiful sunny day, and I finally had a cardboard basket that might have come from the vegetable market, I planned to pick some Schachtelkraut. Since this was a city, one had to be observant as to where one could find these herbs, but I knew a railroad embankment within walking distance from the apartment. It was never mowed and could possibly have these herbs. The apartment itself was the middle floor of a huge building on Herrlein Strasse #3, which was owned by Herr Adalbert Hock. There was one more building and then one was on Wurzburger Street, which led to the bridge under which the train tracks lay. There were two tracks at the bottom of the embankment. One was for eastbound trains and the main train station. The other was for west- and southbound trains and the south train station. At the very top of the embankment was a path, and just beyond the path was fencing that separated private backyard properties from the little-used path and the steep embankment. The path did not end at the beautiful sandstone bridge, but continued on the other side of the bridge, which had dark, shiny cobblestones for a surface. This surface covered the remainder of this important street that led traffic in and out of the city. It led past the military barracks on each side, south of the bridge, in the direction of Schweinheim, which today is part of the city of Aschaffenburg.

I had entered the path right at the bridge and was walking gradually down the embankment. I was just beginning to look for herbs when I saw a train coming slowly from the west and slowing down, as I became aware that it was no ordinary train. It was not a passenger train. The wooden cars were open to the sky, but contained nothing but people from end to end in each car. I could not believe what I was seeing; it was so out of the ordinary. I was mesmerized by the enormity of the human drama, wondering why the train would come to a total halt so that I could not avoid seeing what I was sure I was not meant to see. I focused on one particular woman who was well dressed in a beige outfit that seemed expensive and clashed with her surroundings. She leaned tiredly against the wooden wall of the train car. Her eyes were downcast, absorbed, as it were, in her present situation, which was not yet clear to her, and that she could not do anything about. I thought about the fact that there were no bathrooms. I also thought, "The sun is shining, but what if it were to rain?" All they had was the clothes on their backs. I did not think of counting train cars, but there must have been ten or even twenty. Where had they all come from? I had heard of concentration camps and thought that this was their eventual destination.

Men and women were packed body-to-body so that there was no more room in the cars, and all were standing and silent. It was that very silence that was broken momentarily by the fast, running footsteps that I heard approaching from the west, on the path above. I turned just as a male figure disappeared towards the bridge. I do not recall ever having seen anyone run as fast as that man, and the reason became clear, as right after him came a helmeted and gun-toting German soldier. The soldier had boots on, which slowed him down despite great effort to move as fast as possible, with a German Shepherd pulling on its leash. For a moment I thought, "What if this soldier takes me for an escapee?" But he took little notice of me. They kept running on the path towards the street and disappeared.

I wondered about the man who must have jumped from one of the train cars, and why he jumped just then. Beyond my eyesight, there was a curve in the tracks, and the embankment was the reason the train had slowed enough to allow him to jump. Had there been other reasons? I remembered that in the direction the escaped man ran, there were a series of apartment buildings, that I recently had passed, that were empty. I had passed the cul-de-sac street and noticed that the windows were open with curtains fluttering in the breeze. Doors were not closed. All this looked like people were removed forcibly from these apartments. I was wondering if maybe that man had lived there or knew something about that place to help him possibly find refuge there.

I do not recall hearing a shot. But after another minute or two, the train cars slowly moved forward on their terrible journey, and an unforgettable moment of my shattered childhood rolled under the bridge and left me standing on a steep embankment with an empty basket. I felt so alone, and yet relieved I was not on that train. I knew I would never forget this moment as long as I lived; it was deeply etched into my consciousness. I knew that I was changed, but I did not know just what that might mean for my life. I also wondered if I should even talk about it. Would my aunt believe me, and did she and my uncle know this was happening right near their apartment in Aschaffenburg?

Waiting for Friends (acrylic on paper)

Taking a Bow (acrylic and collage)

15

SS OFFICERS AT THE DOOR

SS Officers.

WHILE I was living at Herrlein Strasse #3, I left early in the morning for school. The primary school I went to was very close by. It was around the corner and then about one block farther. About two years later, I had to walk quite a distance, all across town, to a secondary school, called Gymnasium. This was a grand red sandstone building with a huge playground area that intimidated me greatly. I was not one to play ball with the other boys. I and one other boy stayed away from all the excitement and leaned against a wall to eat our sandwiches. The recess seemed terribly long to both of us. This boy was very delicate and soft spoken.

At that time, food was already becoming scarce, so what one was given from home was a piece of rye bread with some butter and jam on top. This was cut in half and then laid jam side to jam side. This was wrapped in newspaper or some other paper and put in a paper bag. Possibly an apple was added. Almost no one had white bread or rolls. I remember a boy who did have white bread with a great crust. He was the son of a baker. He would pull pieces off the *stollen* (rolls) he had and hold these way up high; we all jumped up to see if we could reach it. It was such a relief to get one of these pieces during recess. If you didn't, it resulted in disappointment.

During this time, in late fall, I noticed a German soldier standing across the street from our house entrance, taking notes in a little booklet. I did not think much about it, but I did wonder what on earth could be interesting enough in that spot that some person was standing there and taking notes. And even after school, when I came home, he was still there, and I then wondered where he had gone to urinate during that time.

On one of those days when he was not standing across the street, I happened to be all alone in the apartment. I was probably laboring over my mathematics, which I was not good at. The doorbell rang. It had never rung before, so this was startling in itself, but I went to the apartment door and opened it.

Whoa! What a sight! There were two spit-and-polished SS officers standing at attention with a German Shepherd at their side. He was a beautiful dog—all perfect, like the officers themselves. They saluted, which surprised me even more. Here were two officers with a dog, outside the apartment. "Yes?" I said (in German, of course). One of the officers said that he wondered if I was interested in being traded for a German soldier, who was being held in the United States as a prisoner. Well, I had never thought of such an idea and was startled by this.

Standing there alone in front of these two soldiers with a dog was just so strange. What if I said yes without consulting Tante Lizzy or Uncle Otto? It was just so foreign to my mind! I then immediately said, "No! I am a student here, and I expect to finish my studies here at the Gymnasium." I do not remember what they said next, but then they saluted, turned, and walked down the steps. It was with great relief that I closed the apartment door. I went straight to the toilet. I was greatly relieved that they had not taken me with them, and that I would be able to talk to Uncle Otto and Tante Lizzy to see what they would think of the situation. Can you imagine having to make such a decision at that age? At some point, I was also told by the SS that I would have to report to them whenever I was planning to go to Hausa, and to tell them how long I expected to be gone. They said I should also report to them after I came back from the village.

Another strange thing was that, in the village, there was a man who was not a native of the village. This man would come every day in the afternoon, right after mealtime, to buy a glass of Schnapps. When he came, Mama Karolina would call me if I was within hearing distance and ask me to come into the room where she had given this man the Schnapps. She said I should say hello to him. It always seemed so odd that this stranger should show any interest in me. It never occurred to me that his whole job in the village was simply to see if I was still there. This occurred to me many years after the war was over. I was in Brooklyn College when I was relating this story to a fellow student. The presence of this man meant that the SS always knew where I was, the entire time they were in power.

Tree (watercolor and pen)

My Cousin Walter as a Young Man.

I had started my formal education in Aschaffenburg by going to Volkschule for two years. Now that I was ten years old, and in fifth grade, I had the option of going to the *Gymnasium*, for classical education, or to the *Realschule*, to learn business-type trade skills and English. Tante Lizzy and Uncle Otto decided I would go to the Gymnasium, where Latin was taught. They felt this was important in case I should want to become a Catholic priest when I grew up.

The first year in the Gymnasium went pretty well. It was during this time, however, that the bombing had begun. I remember that the first bomb that came down was quite far from our house. Tante Lizzy made a point of taking me to see the house that it had hit. Tante Lizzy, and others, said that it was an incendiary bomb, which should have caused a fire, but had not exploded properly. The bomb was a six- or eight-sided metal canister, about a foot long. Everyone I saw around there had a serious expression on their face, and everyone was silent. They all stepped carefully over the debris scattered on the floor of the house.

Tante Lizzy and I walked back through the city, over the train tracks and back to our house. She was always reserved, and wrapped up in her own thoughts, and was tall and elegant. One thing I do remember is that she always spat on the sidewalk when we passed the children's hospital or the doctor's office, to show disrespect for them. She blamed them for the death of her children. But I think her silence as she walked with me let me know that people were scared, and that they were scared of what they might say and who might hear them.

Soon after that, my cousin Walter came to live with us, and we shared a room. Walter was older than me, and had attended a different Gymnasium. He was put into the class above me, and soon started to learn Greek. During this time, the number of bombings increased very quickly. Some residents were assigned to patrol, to make sure no lights were showing in people's windows. I was too young for this, but Walter was not, so he had to run out into the streets when the bombings started, instead of heading for shelter in the cellar as the rest of us did. I did not envy poor Walter.

It was not a pleasant experience; if the attack came at night, we had to get dressed as quickly as possible and dash for the cellar. The windows had sandbags in front of them to protect from flying debris like stones and other heavy objects. Among those of us that were assembled in the cellar one night were Fraülein Hock, the daughter of the owner of the house; and her friend, Herr Buckle (this was not his real name, which I never knew). Also with us were Tante Lizzy and Uncle Otto. We heard planes overhead, and we heard the crash of bombs. There were many of them because the enemy was carpet bombing all across the city. The explosions of the bombs became louder and closer together. There was a rumbling noise I had never heard before.

The noise sounded like a heavy truck was bearing down on us with tremendous speed. I felt in my bones that this was it, and the compression of air above us as the bomb descended was unbearable. My ears hurt. I know the color must have drained out of my face, and I think I held my breath. And then it was right there, so loud, such an impact! The walls shook. The window cracked. Pieces of wood fell, and a big cloud of dust came down from the ceiling. The floor shattered, and a wall behind me partially collapsed. Something loudly crashed to the floor in the room behind that wall. All this happened in an instant, but then there was silence. I listened for the next sound, but there was nothing else—the planes had moved on.

I was shaken, but I walked over to Tante Lizzy and put my hand on her arm and just looked at her. I said nothing, and she in return said nothing. Instead, she looked over at Uncle Otto and he looked back at both of us. I really do not know what I could have or should have said. I think I was trying to bridge the gap between the reserved, elegant adult and the little kid, who was glad we had all survived. I was glad that Tante Lizzy had survived. I had never touched her before. She had never touched me much, either. I saw that Fraülein Hock smiled, or perhaps grinned.

Suddenly, the door flung open, and Walter came into the room. He flattened his body against the stone wall of the cellar and was white as a sheet. He was all out of breath, and his lips were tightly pressed together. I wondered exactly where he had been outside when the bomb fell. Maybe he was just feet away from the actual point of impact. Had stones from the pavement whizzed past his head? I never dared to ask him.

We waited for the "all clear" sirens that told us we could come out of the cellar. Fraülein Hock said, "I think we can go upstairs now and see how much damage was done to the house. Maybe we can even get some sleep tonight, if there are no further attacks."

Silently we filed upstairs. On the stairs to the second floor, there were crunchy sounds underfoot—pieces of plaster from the wall had come loose, but it was difficult to tell in the dark. Then, on the landing, there was the distinctly slippery sound of broken glass from the big window that brought light into the stairwell during the daytime. When I got to my bed, I felt cold air. I touched my bed—it was full of glass shards. It was too dark to tell how much glass, but I knew I could not go back to bed, not tonight. The apartment was not livable anymore. I cannot now recall what we did the rest of the night, but in the nights following, we slept in the cellar of my Uncle's school. He was a professor in a teacher's school some blocks away. During the day, we stayed in our apartment, wearing our coats.

The morning after that devastating bomb hit, somehow I thought that I would not go to school as usual, but Tante Lizzy said, "Get your school bag and get ready for school." My eyes widened, but I did as I was told. This was how I got to see the bomb crater out in the street. Just ten feet away from me was a crater a grown man could have stood in, head level with the street.

When I think of what today's bombs could do, I thank my lucky stars that technology had not come along as far back then. I moved along, and wondered what the rest of the city looked like. After I turned right, away from Herrlein Strasse, I could see whole facades of houses collapsed into the street. Some houses were like missing teeth in the mouth of the city. Women dressed in black were in the street to see if there was anything salvageable in the debris. I was the only kid on the street.

The women looked at me in wonder. It felt strange. The further I walked, the worse it got. Then I came upon places that looked like nothing had happened the night before, but when I got to the Gymnasium, there was no building!

All that was there were piles of rubble. There would never be another school day in that location. I never saw any of the boys from my class there ever again. I wondered why I was the only child who had come on this walk through the rubble of Aschaffenburg. From this spot next to the rubble of the Gymnasium I could see the castle, and the beautiful red sandstone building was also heavily damaged; the tower roofs were gone. Metal and wood beams reached into the gray sky as if they were reaching for their lost hats. My beloved *schloss*, my castle, was gone, and I shivered on the cold November day. My life, my world had collapsed. I was small and alone. What would happen to me now?

Being Bombed (wood block print). Here the child in the chair is me. The man standing over, with his hand on my head, is is my Uncle Otto. The woman facing us is Tante Lizzy

WHEN THE AMERICANS CAME

W HEN the war ended, I had been living in Hausa since the time
that Aschaffenburg was destroyed. Uncle Otto and Tante Lizzy
had also come to Hausa. Everyone in Hausa was expecting the arrival
of the Americans. School in Hausa had continued until Germany capit-
ulated. Then, the teacher just left. He had been appointed by the Nazi
government, so he was no longer paid.

One morning, Ernst, a boy from next door, came running in saying
that the Americans were expected to come that morning to Hausa. I do
not know how he knew this. He did know that we had a small window
on the north side of the hayloft, and another one even higher up in the
barn. He urged me to follow him up to one of these windows to watch
for the American trucks that were coming over the mountain in the
northwest. He was not sure which route they would take, but both could
be seen from these unglazed windows.

After looking out for a while and wondering what the Americans
might be like, and being glad that it was not going to be the Russians,
Ernst yelled, "Oh, look! Here they come! I wonder how many trucks will
come into Hausa and how long they are going to stay here!"

"I don't think they'll stay long. There is nothing for them to do here,"
I replied.

By that time, the first trucks were rumbling into the main street of
the village. There was no longer any reason to be up under the roof of
the barn when the activity was now on the ground. We had to be careful
climbing down the long ladder from the top of the barn to the ground
level. A false move could result in a major accident. When we reached

the bottom, Ernst decided to run home. His house was just on the other side of our barn.

By the time I got into the house, there were already *Amis* in the wirtschaft. They did not seem friendly at all due to their reserved behavior, and especially because they held long, shiny, steel wands that looked dangerous. Much later, I learned that those were cattle prods. Uncle Ottmar looked overwhelmed, maybe even scared. Karolina was also there, with her lips pressed together. It looked like serious business was going on. It was clear that Ottmar was not in control. And I wondered if I would be better off anywhere else but right there. The American soldier with the decorated shoulders looked at me and nodded to the door.

I took the hint and slunk out into the yard. There, other soldiers were busy setting up things and examining the place to see what was there and how it might be of use to them. There was also a truck. When the rear door was let down, I could see it was a food truck. A soldier was taking cardboard boxes down. When he opened one of the boxes, I saw purple trays that held bright red apples in purple tissue paper. They all looked very much alike. I had never seen anything like that. And what was even stranger to me was that it was spring, definitely not apple season. In Hausa, you only had apples in the fall. Then, all sorts of things were made out of apples. And the apples were never perfect like these were.

Well, I must have looked as if I wanted one of these perfect apples because the soldier in charge of them held one out towards me and smiled. He might have said in English, "Do you want an apple, kid?" To which I nodded. I knew his intention and the word "apple" sounded a lot like the German word *"apfel,"* so it was easy to comprehend. I reached for it and expected to taste a really good apple taste when I bit into it. On the contrary, I made a face and thought, "Yech! This is a mealy apple!" I had never had an apple that was mealy before. It made me wonder why all that care had been bestowed on these mealy apples. They looked good, but did not give you that juicy joy that a good ripe apple should give you. And that made me wonder what other surprising American things I would discover. Even at that age, I made value judgments. Right there, that apple became a nasty cultural disappointment instead of a delicious treat. I thought, "When I finally get to the United States, I'm going to have to learn a lot of stuff that I would rather do without." But since I could not speak any English, I kept silent and soon got further unpleasant news.

The Americans had taken over the house and had determined that Karolina would sleep in the straw in the barn. I would sleep there, unless I would go to Karolina's step sister's house, and sleep there. Klothilda had room for me, and I would have a bed there. After looking at the place where Karolina was expecting to stay the night, I left for Klothilda's house up the street.

She had two daughters slightly younger than me. Her husband had been killed in the war. Her father and mother had died years before. It was her father whom I had called Herrla years ago, when he pulled me around in a little wagon. He was my babysitter at a time when Karolina could not have me around because she had work to do.

Well, curfew started at 6:00 p.m. and lasted until about 8:00 a.m. Both of these times were hard on the villagers, as they had lots of work to do. Starting late and stopping early meant some work could just not fit into a day. For farmers depending on the weather, that was a problem. The good thing was that this situation did not last long. Hausa was of no importance to the Americans. They had to get on their way east. I do not think it was longer than a week that the Americans stayed there.

When we all were finally allowed into the house, it became clear that the soldiers and officers had not obeyed the Off Limits sign Uncle Otto had put on the door of the storage room. That room, on the second story, was right next door to Uncle Otto's room. Apparently, because he could speak English, he had been allowed to stay in the house. Perhaps he had been used as an interpreter. Well, all the bread loaves Karolina had baked were gone, as were the very good smoked ham and the eggs that had been saved in cut-up straw.

I don't remember just how we managed to eat in the following months. People must have helped us with canned meats and veggies. We had sauerkraut and there were potatoes in the cellar. The chickens still laid eggs, but it was too early to have new vegetables in the garden at that time of year. There was flour from last year's harvest and there was milk from the cows. Karolina managed somehow.

I wonder what Baraska was doing during the time the Americans were in the village. I am sure she and the other Poles were interviewed by the Americans, and then that information was passed on to the Russians, so they knew where to find those people, whom they considered their spoils of the war. Eventually, the Russians came and got Baraska. I do not know whether Ottmar paid Baraska from the end of the war until then, or if she chose to work for food. She had no resources of her own to feed herself and her two children. Perhaps she came to work on her own terms.

Attic Still Life (watercolor)

18

HAUSA IN DEFEAT

I wondered how I would feel when I would have to leave Hausa. I saw how the new Germany was beginning. We had all seen the arrival of the Americans in Hausa. The first thing that happened was that the American soldiers singled out our house and wirtschaft as the place from which they would command the rest of the village. That was because our guest rooms could accommodate a lot of soldiers at once.

I hoped Uncle Ottmar would not come to any harm. He was told what conditions the American military demanded of him and Karolina. After a soldier had given me a mealy apple, I wondered, "If they have such mealy apples in the United States, why would I want to go there?" I wondered what other things in the that country looked great but gave no satisfaction.

I felt sorry for Mama Karolina. Not only for having to sleep in the hay, but also for having her own property commandeered. It showed me that defeat in war can bring many changes, and none for the better.

The war had ended; I was thirteen then. Germany barely functioned as a country; it had been divided into sectors. Hausa was in the American Sector with the rest of Bavaria. There were trains, mostly on the slowest routes that had not been demolished. All Germans now knew what some had known all along. People were prepared for a new, divided Germany. All those not in the Russian sector heaved a sigh of relief. We heard about the Marshall Plan. We hoped that we would knit our country back together. The US. soldiers had arrived.

The Nazi flags had been burned. (I did not see it happen, but it must have happened!) The Bavarian white-and-blue flags made a shy appearance here and there. The outfit Karolina had made for me out of one of those flags was now an embarrassment. It lay lonely in some drawer; I never thought of it. The farm labor went on as best as could be done without Baraska. Fritz worked very hard. Neighbors helped each other; war widows wrecked their bodies trying to do men's work.

My mother had again sent some packages to Karolina containing sugar, coffee, chocolate, and cocoa powder. Later, I learned that she also sent some to her brother in Yugoslavia. He had several children and had been asking for help from my mother. Coffee, especially, was very welcomed, as there was none to be had in Germany. Letters that my father had written were now no longer covered with black redactions. Baraska had been taken away by the Russians and I was in limbo, waiting to be called by my parents to come back to them.

Edge of the Forest (watercolor)

19

MY DEPARTURE FROM GERMANY

My last day in Hausa, 1946.

WHILE back in Hausa, I had to return to the volkschule, because that was the only school that was there. At this school, all the grades were in one room. Uncle Otto and Tante Lizzy had gone back to Aschaffenburg to start their lives there again. I and others were wondering when I was going to hear from my parents to ask that I should come back, and in what manner. We wondered why it took so long. Later I learned that my parents were asking the military to arrange my transport back to them. No doubt this ended up saving my parents a lot of money and time.

After two years, the letter came. It said that I was to report to military barracks in the Frankfurt area at a certain time, and so I had to face ending my childhood, a childhood that had not prepared me for such a drastic change.

It was late summer or early fall in 1946 when I had to leave Hausa. I remember the weather was pleasant and nice for traveling. People were wearing summer clothes. A lot of the details of that time period are somewhat vague in my mind. I think I was engrossed in the enormousness of the changes that were facing me. After all, I was leaving everything and everyone I knew and loved. And I would most likely never see Hausa ever again. My life up to that point would become just memory.

Karolina had to get used to me leaving. Ottmar had to get used to me leaving. They had, after all, invested so much of their time and their feelings in me. They had not had their own children, but they had parented me, and we loved each other. Yet my parents in Brooklyn had the legal authority to claim me, and so I had no choice. I really wanted to stay.

Perhaps Uncle Ottmar and Uncle Otto in Aschaffenburg were in touch by mail to determine how best to get me to Frankfurt at the right time. It made sense that I would get to Aschaffenburg first. From there, trains were frequent enough to get me to Frankfurt at the right time. Also, Uncle Otto could accompany me to deliver me to the right place at the right time. This was important to me as I had no knowledge of Frankfurt at all.

After all this was agreed upon, Uncle Ottmar was free to schedule the day of my departure from Hausa. He outdid himself to make my departure a near-royal event. Karolina did her part by getting a suitcase ready for me and deciding what to put in it. Perhaps she packed some cured ham and bread.

Although it could not have been a Sunday (for transportation was not available on weekends), I was dressed as if it were. My fairly-new suit, good socks, and best shoes—ones that fit—made me look and feel important. But I also felt apprehensive. It helped to have boys my age come and hang out by the front door, where I was waiting for someone or something to take me away. They wanted to see how I was taking this leaving-never-to-be-seen-again. Were they jealous of me going on a trip? I must have been asked many times if I would come back. This I could not know, and I said so. We were photographed at this door.

Around 2 p.m., a wagon for horses was pushed into place—in the middle of the street—by people I had never seen before. The excitement was building. Many shook my hand and wished me well. Then, two horses were paraded out and attached to the wagon. I had never seen these beautiful horses before. Ottmar must have ordered them from a neighboring village.

I was motioned to climb up and sit on the blanket-covered board that lay across the two sides of the wagon. I sat next to someone I didn't know. Neither Ottmar nor Karolina came along. I was alone with strangers. After looking back and waving, I had to turn forward and face my future by myself. The wagon took me to Würzburg, where I boarded the train to Aschaffenburg, a trip on which I was all alone. All alone! Can you imagine? The world had conspired to make me the loneliest boy in it.

In Aschaffenburg, Tante Lizzy was there to find me and bring me to Herrlein Strasse #3. I carried my valise all the way there. It was a long walk, and I switched hands often on the way.

It seemed that their formerly very large apartment was now smaller, and the front two rooms housed another person. Since so many places had been bombed, space was at a premium in cities all over Germany. Being with Tante Lizzy and Uncle Otto was good. I was with people who had cared for me. They had helped educate me, and I was thankful to them that I had experienced city life. I had seen theater; I had been exposed to a famous artist; and they had books, many of which they had read. They represented culture beyond the pig sty. The air seemed richer there. I was so thankful for what they had given me.

When we left for Frankfurt, Uncle Otto carried my suitcase to the train station. We had to leave early because we had to be there by a specific time, and Uncle Otto had to be back in Aschaffenburg on the same day. After we got to Frankfurt, we had to take a bus to the southern border of the city. Even Uncle Otto had never been in that part of Frankfurt. We could see the military buildings, and an American Flag was flying at the entrance. The American Occupation military had adopted this complex to not only house its soldiers, but also to collect any and all persons who were scheduled to be brought to the United States. There were many others living there. Across the street was a field of grain growing. So we were literally at the very edge of the city. These buildings were just like the military buildings in Aschaffenburg; none of them had been destroyed. I think the American High Command must have realized they would be needing those buildings when they arrived there.

After Uncle Otto had delivered me, he had to leave. Tante Lizzy wanted him back in the apartment that evening. He may have had to go and teach at his school. Also, Lizzy, as far as I could tell, no longer had a maid.

As soon as Uncle Otto had left, one of the soldiers asked me to open my shirt so he could throw white powder on me. I took this to mean they were afraid I had lice. They also told me they would prepare an American Passport for me, taking whatever papers I had from Germany. They told me to go find a certain room that I would be staying in. I did find this room and I hoped to find someone who would help me understand what was going on and when there was going to be some food.

There was a man who could speak both German and English. He made sure I got some food. In the morning, he got me going to the dining hall where I first saw American breakfast foods. This was my first experience of going with a tray along a line and picking out things to eat.

There were other Americans who had been stuck in Germany during the war besides me. I made the acquaintance of a middle-aged man who was planning to go to Massachusetts. He had plans to work in a shoe factory. We shared a room. We stayed there several weeks, and I became accustomed to eating American food. However, being among so many people I did not know was very hard for me. Nothing had prepared me for this situation. Also, I had no idea how long I was going to be in that unhappy place. And it was boring. I had nothing to do and no money.

Uncle Otto came one day on a surprise visit. I certainly was not expecting him! We went for a brief walk. In the process I spied a bowl of fruit in the only store that was to be seen in the area. I had never seen such perfectly rounded scoops of fruit. I could not imagine from what kind of larger fruit they were carved. I don't think the store had anything but that. Of course I wanted some! I begged Uncle Otto to see if he could buy me a little of that fabulous item. He relented. I do not think it cost very much of the devalued German Mark. I loved the taste and was told that it was watermelon. I had never even heard of this fruit nor how it was grown. Later, I thought that this store had watermelon because it was so close to the barracks occupied by Americans.

I was grateful that I could have tasted such a delicious American fruit while still in Germany. Uncle Otto and I hugged, which we had never done before. Then he continued on down the street to a place where he could get a trolley car to bring him back to the train station. He wiped his eyes as he left, and so did I. As far as I knew, this was my very last contact with him and any of the people who had figured into my childhood.

I was left alone again. It might have been a week that passed before I learned that, on the next day, we would leave. It was early October. After breakfast, we walked to the very end of the property and climbed up the steep embankment to the train tracks. There was a train on the tracks, and we found seats. I made sure I stayed close to the man who could make sure I understood what was going on. We were off to Bremerhaven. The trip there became a lost memory.

The ship was called the SS Marine Marlin. I came to understand that we were on a troop ship. That is why there were six or seven berths from bottom to top. I was afraid to be so high up and was able to find a berth midway. I must have been told by someone to find a way to tie my suitcase to one of the metal pipes that held the berths. This was because the suitcase might have slid away when the ship was tossed by the waves, once we were on the high seas. And indeed there were very high waves, but I loved standing high up in the open air! And I loved watching the ship dive into the deep valleys of the water and then climb up the next mountain, while I held on for dear life as the spray drenched me. I was the only one who did this rather dangerous thing. Eventually, I realized if I should ever lose my grip, I would be a goner, and no one would be able to help me. I soon looked up at some navy men standing above me, and they looked down on me and motioned for me to back up some. I realized they were right, and found a somewhat safer place to experience the terror of the waves.

When eventually the skies cleared and the water calmed, people started to point at distant white clouds and said that that's where New York would show up. I began to imagine what it might be like to meet the parents I did not know. What had they done for me? And my sister—a girl who knew nothing about how I grew up—how could she have any empathy for me? I resolved to be as polite as I could be and to try to agree with whatever might be asked of me. I figured they, too, might have all sorts of feelings about getting reunited with a son they had cast away, only to find that they had sent him into a war zone. Now it was just a day away from when I would actually meet them.

The next day, the ship, holding thousands of people, docked in New Jersey.

Garden Plant (watercolor)

20

MY NEW FAMILY IN BROOKLYN

*Mother, Helen, and Father at the World's
Fair in 1939 or 1940.*

WHEN I arrived in New Jersey, it was October 12, 1946. I was picked up by my mother and two men. One of the men was Mr. Mitchell, a family friend without whom Mother would not have been able to retrieve me. It must have been near noon. It took a long time before I actually left the ship. I was afraid to get off the ship. I was afraid of meeting my family. My mother had, after all, sent me away when I was a baby. And this was to a place that soon became a war zone. These thoughts gave me pause. What if some new emergency would come up that would end up with me being sent away again? Where would this new place be? And here I was, in a country whose language I did not understand. These kinds of thoughts made me leery of getting off the boat. I stood on one of the upper decks for a long time, looking and waiting for someone to come up and get me. Someone eventually came by and told me I had to get off the ship. I may have been the last person to get off the SS Marine Marlin in New Jersey that day.

Hesitantly, I set foot on the blacktop. There I stood with lots of people until I saw a woman coming towards me. I had seen photos of this woman in Germany. These photos were taken on Sundays, because everyone had very nice Sunday-type clothes on. There even had been photos of my sister, Helen. In them, she had lacey dresses on. At some point I learned that some of the photos had been taken at the 1939-1940 World's Fair.

My new mother came close, embraced me, and called me "my son." At this point I flinched. How dare this strange person call me her son? I did not feel I was her son. I was the son of Mama Karolina. She had raised me, and she was entitled to call me her son, not this strange woman. Of course, from my new mother's point of view, what else could she have called me? I had never seen the two men in photos and wondered who they were. I did not see anyone who looked like the photo of my father. After the greetings were over, one of the men motioned that we had to get going. He turned out to be the driver of a black car, toward which he urged us on. I had never been in a private car before. No one in Germany that I knew had owned a car. No one in the little village of Hausa had a car. No one would have been able to afford such luxury. And then there was the fact that very few cars existed in Germany at this time, because of the fact that the war had only allowed production of war materials.

The trip to 327 Lewis Avenue in Brooklyn was very novel to me. It was getting dark already, shortly after we left the area where the ship had docked. We must have gone through a tunnel and were on a ferry and possibly a second tunnel or ferry. It was almost as if the driver had selected a route that was meant to impress me.

Eventually, we came to a stop in the dark in front of some store windows. There was a door beside the store entrance. For this door, my new mother had a key. There was a hallway and I saw a staircase going up. There was an electric light, yet it all seemed dark to me, and scary too.

The hall led to another door on the left, and this turned out to be the kitchen behind the butcher store. There was my sister Helen. Since she was four-and-a-half-years older than me, she was now a grown woman of eighteen, and I was a smallish fourteen-year-old boy. I felt no relationship to this person, and there was only distance between us. There was another person there whom I never saw again. He, apparently, was a family friend. He was a very light-skinned person with kinky hair. My father was nowhere to be seen because he was upstairs in bed. I found this out later as I was led to my bedroom upstairs. My room faced the street, and an electric sign, which was on, was for the liquor store next door.

In the morning, I was shown more about the store, and I started to learn a little about everything that had to be done in it. I soon was put to good use carrying groceries from the store to the homes of shoppers from the neighborhood. Mother, of course, knew all her customers by name. And she called them by their married and family names. I, however, had no idea who was who. I mean no disrespect, but for the longest time, I could not tell one black woman from another.

Helen had a job in Manhattan. She had to walk from the store to the 8th Avenue subway. This was a fairly long walk and Helen was not eager to walk this long walk twice every day. This was especially true in the winter time when it got dark early. Helen was not happy living in that neighborhood. She worked for the New York Life Insurance Company. She took shorthand notes for several bosses in that company, and then typed out the letters.

Helen seemed interested in a man who worked in the Bohak's Grocery Store one block away. My mother was very much against this interest as he was a married man. At least this is what I understood to be the case. But I had my own worries and did not really understand anything that went on with my sister.

After about a year, in the summer, Mother agreed with Helen that she could go on trips and take me with her, so I could see some other parts of this country. Helen wanted to visit a girl friend of hers who had gotten married to someone who had a job at the Ford Motor Company in Detroit. So that's where we went. It might have been on that trip that we also went to Niagara Falls. That was spectacular! The only thing I remember from Detroit was that we had melted cheese sandwiches at Helen's friend's. We went by bus on these trips.

My mother kept the butcher store for a number of years after my father died at King's Hospital. I had been very unhappy over the fact that my father was a bedridden man. I had hoped for a father who would teach me things. This, my father could not do. He, like my mother, had no education, beyond the fact that he was a licensed butcher, having learned his trade in Germany. This is where, I am sure, he learned how to kill animals for the purpose of making meat for sale in stores. In this country, all that was handled by corporations from which he bought pieces of animals, including specific organs, such as livers, stomachs, and entrails. Pig entrails are called chitterlings. These were often bought at our butcher store. Another organ often bought was hog maws. Those are pig stomachs. Mother was not sure how these were prepared by the ladies who bought them; she never prepared them. We often had kidneys or liver. I did like liver with bacon. I also liked bacon and eggs. My mother was also very good at baking things; she had learned to do this in Slovenia. Her baked goods were my favorite.

After my father died while I was still at Halsey Junior High, my mother tried to work the store by herself, which she had essentially been doing. This proved too difficult, so she hired a man who was quite okay. When he no longer wanted to work, Mother tried another man. This man was very awkward. Also, his hands were never easy to look at, for he had long dirty fingernails; for a butcher, it's not a good idea. He eventually was let go, and Mother decided to close the store and sell the house.

From there we moved to Shepherd Avenue. This was in the East New York neighborhood of Brooklyn. Helen was extremely pleased to be away from Bedford Stuyvesant, and she felt safer on the train to work. Mother also found work, at the Metropolitan Life Insurance Company. First she worked in the kitchen, which she hated. Later, she was employed as a courier. And I benefited as well because, in the summer, I was employed in moving the applications of people who had died to an area I called "The Destruction Department..

One pretty awful thing happened with our beloved dog, Fuzzy, whom Mother had had for a very long time. While we had the store, we could just open the back door and Fuzzy could relieve himself in the backyard. When he was cooped up alone all day in our new apartment with no direct ground-level escape to the outdoors, it became a problem, and Mother was not willing to allow for excrement or even pee on the linoleum of the kitchen. I had hoped he could use newspapers, but he did not adapt.

Mother with Fluffy, me, and Helen.

Poor Fuzzy was beaten by Mother and life became a misery. He held his urine so often that he ruined his aging kidneys, and Mother made me take him to the veterinarian to be killed. I had to carry him in my arms as he could no longer walk because of the pain in his kidneys. I was furious that I had to do this. Me, who loved the dog so much. I will never forget that long walk with Fuzzy in my arms. That alone was an affront to my sensibilities, but the honks from the truck drivers were another unexpected element from a world into which I did not easily fit.

21

MY MOTHER DID THE BEST SHE COULD

M Y mother was born in the Austro-Hungarian Empire. During that time, Austria was encouraging its German-speaking citizens to migrate into Slavic-speaking territories. This must have happened to my mother's forebears. As far as I know, at home, Mother's parents and siblings spoke a Germanic dialect that they called *Gottscheberisch*. But apparently, she also understood, and maybe spoke, Slovenian. She read occasional letters from her brother, Ivan, who remained in Slovenia and was moved around into various areas by Josip "Tito" Broz's government as a forester. This resulted in some of his children to think of themselves as Slovenians, others as Bosnians, and still others as Croatians.

Mother's birth name was Amalia Turk and she was either the second or third child of her parents. There was an older sister named Mary, who came to the United States, the brother Ivan, also called "John" by Mother, and a younger sister named Anna, who eventually emigrated to far-west Canada as a mail-order bride, to marry someone from the same area she came from. My mother's mother died from tuberculosis. I do not know how old my mother was when her mother died, but I know that she and her sister were extremely annoyed that their father married, less than six months later, a widow whom he had been seeing during his wife's illness. This widow already had five children of her own, who came with her to their house. It is easy to see that this was really an untenable situation all the way around. "We were always blamed for everything," my mother said many times to me when I was trying to get some information out of her, which was never easy. She did say that Mary, the oldest, left as soon as she could to get to the U.S.

Mary was to send money for my mother as soon as she could, and this happened. Mary also got my mother a job as a cleaning lady for a Jewish family in Brooklyn. Mother then left as soon as passage could be booked. She had no regrets leaving tiny Podpreska, the village that was too small to hold her.

I, at some point, visited Podpreska. My cousin Ivan, a "ladies' man," drove me there after I arrived at the nearest train station. The house where my mother had been born had been demolished, and a newer one had been built farther back on the lot. A garden was now where the birth house had stood. It was indeed a very small community, and close to the Croatian border. There was only Draga, the next community, where Mother had to walk to school. In the cemetery between the two towns was a gravestone for her brother's wife, whom I never knew, but I sang a song over her grave even though I felt somewhat foolish doing it.

After Mother came to the United States, which apparently was via Hamburg, she worked as a maid in Jewish households. At some point she met my father, Karl Alfons Volk, in the Yorktown area of Manhattan, where dances were held regularly for the German community. After their marriage, they eventually started their own butcher shop in the Bedford Stuyvesant area of Brooklyn. Father had been working for other butcher shops, for which he bought the meat from the wholesale market in downtown Brooklyn. Mother worked in the store when not employed elsewhere. During that time, the Depression held sway and sales alone could not pay the rent and other bills. Some of the bills came from the fact that my sister had infantile paralysis, which shortened one of her legs for life. Therefore, my mother was determined to work outside the house to earn enough money to keep them afloat. She got a job in Macy's department store collecting money from the various cash registers in the store. There was no way that she could have a baby and that job. My father, I was told by Aunt Anna later, had come home crying to Mother to intercede and prevent my being sent to his brothers in Germany; but that failed. My mother told my father, "If you do not agree to send this baby to Germany, I will leave you, take our daughter with me, and leave you alone to manage the store." This ultimatum forced my father to acquiesce to her determination. I was brought to the S.S. Bremen and handed over to the ship's nurse, and departed in July of 1933. This was before my first birthday, which was on August 15th of that year. I did not return to the United States until 1947, after the war had ended.

Upon my return, I did not know a word of English, other than "chocolate," which I could not spell. Perhaps I knew "please" and "thank you." I am not sure my sister Helen was happy to see me. She was five-years old when I was sent to Germany and was raised as an only child all those fourteen years. We had no memories of a common childhood, so we never really bonded as a result. She was now eighteen, and I was fourteen.

After my return, Mother had to find a public school for me. She had no idea what to do and made several odd trips to schools clearly not meant for me. One was an all-girls school on Eastern Parkway. I was so embarrassed. She was thinking high school, because I had been in the Gymnasium in Germany; here, I was of junior high age. Finally she got permission to enroll me in Halsey Junior High, one block away from Stuyvesant Avenue. I could take the Halsey Avenue trolley very close to my new school. There was a school closer to me on Lewis Avenue, but it was a black school. I had never seen a black person before moving to the United States and, frankly, was too afraid to go there.

While I went to Halsey Junior High, my mother worked in the butcher store, buying all the meat and vegetables that were delivered by Mr. Mitchell. Father was laid up in bed upstairs with an oxygen tank that was used on and off. So Mother also had to cook for us and feed my father. Every so often, a doctor would look in on my father. These bills also had to be paid.

The apartment above the store was laid out in a railroad design. One had to go through all the rooms to get from the back to the front of the apartment. This did not allow for a lot of privacy, and would never be the layout of a German apartment. So sometimes I heard my mother ask my father, "Do you want that master bath?" And I wondered what that was. Then, no bath followed, but my mother's hand was under the covers. I eventually understood that what she meant was the word "masturbate." That was another way my mother took care of my father during his illness.

I do not think it was much longer than a year after I arrived in this country when my father was taken to Kings County Hospital. Then, I often had to go from school to the hospital to visit him. Mother had to tend to the store. I had not fully realized how sick my father was when I first arrived from Germany. I do remember that I was very annoyed that he was laid up in bed and that that was all I knew of him: a sick, helpless person. I had never seen any man lying in bed all day. It made me feel helpless, and I thought that my mother encouraged him to be helpless and dependent on her.

At some point, I said as much to her: "Mom, I think that Pop needs to get out of bed and get into the fresh air and see something outside the bedroom. Why don't you let me take him to Prospect Park?" She agreed to dress him and off we went. Looking back on that, I am amazed at myself as well as both of my parents for going along with that. We had to take two different trolley lines, which meant climbing up and down several steps each time, not to mention the stairs in the house. After we got into the second trolley line, and I realized how difficult it was for my father, I regretted having had such a bad idea. When we got to the park, Father got off the trolley. I think he sat on the bench just long enough until the next trolley came to take us back to the house. I never opened my mouth again and was glad he had not collapsed on me during that outing. Perhaps this was a lesson to teach me to be satisfied with the reality that is, rather than getting into an even worse set of circumstances. It may also have strengthened my belief in my mother—that she really had a better grip on reality than I had.

One day while I was in school, I was called to the principal's office and told that I had to go home right away as something had happened to my father. Well, he had died at Kings County Hospital. Mother was looking into buying a casket and wanted me to go with her. I think she just could not face all those unpleasant things by herself, and she was teaching me what to do for her when she would pass away. She wanted a really nice casket for her husband but something she could afford. Much later in her life, she told me not to buy her an expensive coffin but to get the cheapest one they had. She said it was just a matter of business for the undertaker, who wanted to make money off the grief of the relatives of the deceased member of the family. I listened to her and she got a paper coffin when she died at age eighty-nine. My father was only about fifty-five when he died. I often wondered if I would follow suit and die early. Apparently, I have inherited my mother's genes.

After my father was buried in St. John's Catholic Cemetery in Middle Village, Queens, Mother hired a helper in the butcher store. This gave her some time to go buy meat at the wholesale meat market. Often, I would be sent there to get a liver or a hind of lamb, which I carried on my lap in the trolley car. I was also sent for chickens, hog maws, and chitterlings. Since the store was in a black neighborhood, chitterlings—pig intestines—were selling well. I do not know how they were cooked. In Germany, they were used for sausage casings.

As I had graduated from Halsey Junior High, I now walked from Lewis Avenue to Nostrand Avenue, where Boys' High School was located. It was a long walk but it was good for me. It was a big change, and I liked Boys' High much better than junior high. It was, of course, a step up in maturation. Much more was expected. Intermediate algebra, however, humbled me, and I realized math was not my thing. Literature, biology, and art were my interests instead.

During this time, Mr. Mitchell became a familiar person. He was the vegetable supplier for my mother's store. He also used his Sundays to take my mother, sister, and me on motor car trips. His wife worked on

Sundays in a bakery store. Often, we would end Sunday at their house for dinner. She was an excellent Italian cook and always had delicious cookies for dessert. I do not think there was anything going on between my mother and Mr. Mitchell. Sometimes, Mother would cook for the Mitchells! If it had not been for him, I would never have left the boundaries of the city. So I was very grateful to have him volunteer to take us on outings to the surrounding countrysides.

My mother's treatment of my sister deserves some discussion. There were a number of times when my mother would get physical with my sister, Helen. This, despite the fact that Helen was now working, and was twenty-one years old. It usually had something to do with her choices, or lack thereof, of male companions. It must be remembered that we lived in a near one-hundred-percent black neighborhood. So, there were no white neighbors around with suitable sons of Helen's age, and at work I suppose she dealt mainly with married men, who were her bosses. The other employees were also younger women. Helen went to dances for which my mother was glad, for she was hoping Helen would find a beau. However, coming home from the subway was a potential problem. At times, I was asked to go and meet her at the subway entrance.

When Helen seemed to get serious with a married man at the local grocery chain, Bohak's, Mother was incensed and physically attacked Helen, who had to defend herself with raised arms. There were lots of tears and shrieks on the part of Helen, and loud recriminations from my mother, who repeated many times, "What on earth are you thinking?! He will have a heck of a time getting a divorce. Besides, he will have to pay alimony from his measly job at Bohak's. And you'll be married to a man who could not hold his first marriage together. And with the long hours at his job, you'll be sitting home alone many more times than you'd like."

There may have been more arguments that supported my mother's concerns. Helen did point out that being in this neighborhood, where she was clearly at a disadvantage, eventually led to the sale of the store to a West Indian family. We stayed there less than a year until Mother got a job at the Metropolitan Life Insurance Company, in the kitchen, which she detested. After we moved to Shepherd Avenue in East New York, things between my mother and Helen were a little less stressed. And eventually, Mother left the kitchen of Met Life to work in the offices, for which she brought policy papers from place to place, and had other duties for which writing was not required.

After Fuzzy was put down, Mother picked the upstairs tenants as her next target. They were apparently under rent control, so Mother could not legally raise their rent. There was a mother and maybe a father, and two boys who were a little younger than me. I was studying at Brooklyn College by this time and had a long subway ride each day and a lengthy walk after the subway ride. Often when I came home, Mother would be screaming up the stairs. I do not recall anything she actually said, if there were any words at all. Mother's efforts were directed at them to leave that apartment so that she could rent it out for more money to people of her choosing.

I distanced myself from these goings-on as much as I could, and was glad I was not home that much. I made sure I had plenty of classes, and, if that was not enough, I got hours at the college library so that I had things to do without having to go home. This arrangement was not to Mother's liking, and at some point she went to the offices of Brooklyn College and complained about my hours or some such thing. I do remember being called from class at some point, perhaps it was from Mr. Rothko's art class. This was my introductory class in the art department that counted towards my graduation down the road. I was so humiliated by this intervention in my affairs that I formed a distinct dislike for my mother that lasted quite a long time afterwards. It was the only thing that brought me a little closer to my sister.

I have to mention here that I could only go to college because New York City colleges were free at that time, when the Democrats still had power and people believed that a well-educated population was a boon to the general well-being and wealth of the country. Nowadays, that does not seem to be the case, and young people are saddled with huge college debt, which is a detriment to their mental health and leads to negative feelings about their relationship with this country.

Mother was really glad that I graduated, and to show her happiness, she allowed me to take a trip to the West Coast that included a visit to her sister, Anna, in Calgary. That is where Anna and her husband, Frank, had moved after Frank retired from the mines in Drumheller.

Speaking of Anna, this reminds me of the first time I had met her. It was the time she arrived unannounced in New York City all the way from Alberta. Thank God it was summer, and warm, for in the evening, she called up and said she was someplace in Manhattan. I had no idea where that might be. If she had called from Kennedy Airport, I would have known how to get there from our house on Shepherd Avenue. However, since I had never heard anything positive about her, I was quite cold to her on the phone. Mother was crying, and I really was not sure what that was about.

Anyway, neither of us knew what we could do and we directed Anna to her and Mother's older sister, Mary, who apparently did know that Anna was coming. Eventually, Anna and my mother did meet, and I got to meet my aunt who was the nicest of people. She was not anything like what I had imagined after all the negative things my mother had said about her, if she was mentioned at all. The thing that had rankled my mother was that Anna had not repaid her the money Mother had sent to allow Anna to leave Podpreska, along with all five of their step-siblings. Later, I was so relieved that the relationships between the sisters was cleared up and had a fairly good ending.

22

NOW WHAT, MOTHER?

W E were still living on Lewis Avenue and Mom was still working in the store. Helen was still living with us and working as a stenographer for the New York Life Insurance Company. Father had not yet died. One day I came home from church, and found Mother by my father's bedside. She asked him, "Do you want a master bath?" I wondered what that could be. Apparently, no water was involved. I noticed that my mother had some tissues in her hand. She put her hands under the covers. My father gave me a look I will never forget as I continued through the room. I saw my mother's hands making motions under the covers. I decided that I knew what my mother was doing to my father. In my room, facing the street, I sat on the one chair that fit beside the bed and sorted out what I had just seen. I decided that, since my father had heart disease, my mother was doing him a service to replace vaginal intercourse, which would be a stress on my father's heart that he could ill afford. Of course, I also wondered about the word mother had used. At the time, I had not yet learned the word "masturbate."

Eventually, when I did learn that word in the Brooklyn College Library, I understood that my mother had not learned it correctly. I also thought that it was a kindness my mother wanted to give to my father. At the time, I never wanted to discuss that event with my mother. I would not have had the words, and I would have been too embarrassed. I also reasoned that perhaps the doctor had advised my mother to do this for my father. Or, simply my mother had decided to do this, herself. The time came when father was brought to Kings County Hospital, far away from our neighborhood. Sometimes I went to visit him there. I helped to change the sheets and otherwise make him comfortable. He died there, and I went with my mother to pick a casket and a stone for his grave. Mother selected a grave where she and I could also be buried when our times came. This happened in 1948, a year after I had arrived from Germany. My father was in his fifties. I was fifteen.

After some months had passed, I went to bed one night. My mother came into the room and put the chair near the bed and put her hands under the covers. I was alerted to this, was surprised, and questions flared up in my head. When her hands advanced towards me I moved my body farther to the wall. Her hands advanced towards my groin, and I moved my body away from her hands. I remembered the time she had done this to my father. I remembered my Catholic lessons and feared for myself and for my mother from that point of view also. When I had reached the wall, and there was no place else to go, I sat up. Mother got up and turned to leave. I kicked the chair aside and wanted to hit my mother. I thought for a second how I could do that so it would not show, and I decided a punch in the spine would work. I lifted my arm, crooked my elbow, and hit my mother's spine. She stumbled somewhat forward, towards her bed, and fell on it, crying. I felt sorry for her and for myself that this had happened. I whispered threateningly in her ear, "Don't touch me again!" She wiggled her body. I was surprised again, and went back to my bed.

This did not happen again, but on future nights, I was often remembering this event, and prepared myself for if it were to occur again. I placed the chair in the door, so it would have to be moved by me if anyone were to enter.

I never spoke about this to anyone. I did wonder if it happened to other people as well, and what they might have done other than what I did.

23

THE MOTHERS IN MY LIFE

Mama Karolina.

MY first mother was my Aunt "Mama" Karolina in Hausa. She was born in the village. The house she was born in still stands. However, the present owners, Karolina's niece Gertrude and her husband, would like it to fall down so that they can use the property to build a new house for one of their children when that child is ready to be married. Mama Karolina and her step-sister, Klothilda, are not around anymore, and even if they were, they would have nothing to say about the house they were born in, and neither do I. I did paint a watercolor of it and make a hand-pulled acrylic resist print of it. I call it *Dornroschen*, after the fairy-tale character Sleeping Beauty. In the tale, the princess and the court go to sleep for a hundred years until a prince cuts his way through the brambles of the roses and wakes her with a kiss.

Mama Karolina was a hard-working woman. She worked in the field alongside her husband, Ottmar, and any other help they could get, including me, Baraska, and Fritz. Often, there were only the two of them and the oxen or cows that pulled the wagon or plow. Karolina dressed in the local style of peasant women. They wore indigo blue aprons, skirts, and headkerchiefs. In the summer, the headkerchiefs were white with indigo dots, too small to be called polka dots.

Mama Karolina worked in the house as well as the fields. I remember how the floor of the wirtschaft had to be cleaned each Monday. First, all the ashtrays had to be cleaned. The floor had to be swept. Often, a little water was sprinkled on the floor to make less dust. Other times, pails of water and brushes on long handles were used to wash the floors. Several times a year, the floorboards would have to be oiled. They were of a soft wood and one could get splinters if one was not careful with the cloth one had in one's hand. This work was done on one's hands and knees. I know this because I helped with that work on at least one occasion. When some of the relatives were available, they helped too, including Emma, the daughter of Karolina's cousin. She often was my caretaker. Also often in the house to help was Luisa, another village girl from a large family.

During the Nazi era, we had help from a group of young women who volunteered to work on farms, dressed in blue dresses, red neckerchiefs, and white aprons. That was only during the early and hopeful era of Hitler's reign. Soon, they had to be otherwise employed. Then there were French prisoners of war. We had two different ones, at separate times. Later, somehow, all of these French men disappeared and Ukrainians and Poles were brought in. That's when we got Baraska. She and her husband had two children while their lives were used up in the service of German peasants.

None of this made Karolina work any less. There was always more to do. There were considerations of priorities. Someone had to decide what was going to get done each day and what could be put off for another day. Some things never got done. When there was rain, either the farm work had to be let go, or it just could not wait and someone had to get out into the field in the rain. So time management was a big lesson. I also learned that hard work was the lot of most people, and that some people were always worse off than others. While I was there, I was expected to pull my weight, and I did.

Karolina continued on to raise another brood. You see, when Ottmar had given up the farming and had not produced an heir of his own, my cousin Otto, named the same as my uncle Otto, was called upon to inherit the farm and the beer garden with his wife from a neighboring village. This couple produced two daughters. Their mother died when they were still children, and Mama Karolina stepped back into the role of mother, for these two girls, Eva and Monica. Their father developed epilepsy, and as soon as Eva could drive a tractor, she had to step in and do this part of the farming operation. Their father eventually died of an accident resulting from a seizure, and this made Eva and Monica the owners of the place that was my first home.

When Mama Karolina aged, she developed Alzheimer's and was looked after by the two girls she had raised. During this time, I occasionally visited this village where I had grown up. When Ottmar divided his property, my mother and my sister, Helen, each got some money, but I asked for summertime visits to visit Karolina and the rest of the family. I could not accept any money from the couple who had been my first parents, and I still visit there each year whenever I can.

* * *

Tante Lizzy.

My second mother was Tante Lizzy, the wife of Otto, an older brother of my father. Somewhere along the line of his education, he met Elizabeth Grobholz (Tante Lizzy) from the Palatinate, also known as the Pfalz. She was from a middle-class family and always felt a little less high class than her sisters, who married military men and thus seemed more risen in the social strata. She was definitely a city gal, and she had a maid. That was quite different from Mama Karolina.

Part of the decision to move me to the city of Aschaffenburg was that I was somewhat smaller than other boys my age, and it would not do to make me into a peasant farmer. And, in the meantime, Fritz Konrad had come into the family of Ottmar and Karolina. I'm not sure how or why Fritz came to live with us. Perhaps it was a kind of welfare program in which poor boys and girls were taken from their parents and put into the homes of couples who had no children of their own and needed someone strong to help with field work. He might even have been kidnapped!

It was quite an adjustment to go from Hausa, with three hundred inhabitants, to a city of many thousands. When I was in Volkschule, Tante Lizzy found out that math was not my strong subject, so she had me go to remedial math after school some days. It was great luck that the math teacher had a plum tree in his yard. That helped me count and subtract, especially when I knew I could eat the plums if I got my sums right. This teacher could also draw stick figures and make them climb up the tree and pick plums and put them in baskets. And I loved the way a blank piece of paper could become a beehive of activity. So not only did I learn my sums, I also learned that drawing could be fun and interesting. That was something that appealed to me, and that is one way my aunt Lizzy affected my life path, by sending me to this teacher.

She also taught me manners. She wanted me to know how to shake hands and how to make a bow to her friends. Apparently, she also wanted me to know that one could hold a grudge if one needed to, like the grudge she held against the children's hospital and the doctor's office since giving birth to three boys that all died in infancy. So, I became a substitute child for her, and that was another reason I was moved from the village to the city. But in the summers, I was always glad to go and visit Mama Karolina. I loved to work with her and my uncle Ottmar.

Tante Lizzy cooked meals very differently from the farm ways of Mama Karolina. Lizzy prided herself in culinary skills, and she had help in the preparation of the meals, as well as with the housework. One of the maids I knew best was Lydia. I thought she was so beautiful. I got to eat breakfast with her, and she made my school lunches too. Uncle

Otto would be gone to teach, and Tante Lizzy would still be in bed when I had to get ready for school.

Tante Lizzy made sure I went to the dentist and the physicians, and she accompanied me there. She made sure I got to see some plays and hear some music. So, from that early exposure, I became very fond of theater and dance. In fact, the mother of one of my schoolmates was an actress in the local theater. I envied this schoolmate who appeared at times as a little dwarf in children's plays.

Tante Lizzy also made sure I would get up and get dressed as fast as I could to run into the basement when the sirens blasted us out of our sleep, announcing that we were about to be bombed. We all gathered in one of the cellar rooms. Each one had their chair to wait for the "all clear" siren. The attacks became more and more frequent as the war progressed. The bomb craters became deeper and deeper and closer together. Sometimes fighter planes would go up and try to fight the bombers. One could see the searchlights crisscrossing in the sky, trying to focus on the bombers. I learned to hate war and all it signifies.

My cousin, Walter, had joined us in Aschaffenburg by this time. He wanted to become a priest and was a very good student. I've written about the night he was out on patrol the night a bomb hit right next to our house. A glass jar in the cellar that held precious eggs burst open. We had to eat those eggs in short order, so that they would not spoil. Each bit of food was precious these days, and we often relied on produce from Uncle Ottmar.

Adalbert Hock is remembered in Aschaffenburg. He was a well-known local painter who had done altar paintings in his younger years, and had decorated the Pompejanum, the villa Aschaffenburg has high above the Main River. I admired his ability to paint whatever he wanted. My Aunt Lizzy encouraged me to ask him about my art homework, and he drew three sparrows that looked so life-like to me I thought it was sheer magic. I was hooked on art from then on. So here, too, Tante Lizzy had an effect on my life path.

When Tante Lizzy sent me to school the day after the big bombing, I climbed over ruined houses and hardly knew where the streets were. People were digging out everywhere and there was a calm unreality about it, like it was a movie, and I was a lonely actor in it. My world had crumbled; Aschaffenburg was in ruins.

Uncle Ottmar came soon after and plans were made for us to evacuate to Hausa. I went back with him and, after some time, all the furniture came by train to Trennfeld. We had to take the oxen and make the long journey to Trennfeld to collect the furniture and bring it over the mountains to Hausa.

* * *

Mother.

MY third and biological mother greeted me with a warm embrace in New Jersey. It had taken all day for the thousands of people to get off the boat and be processed. My mother was a stranger to me, and I was not at all sure where I wanted to be. I was not sure if I even wanted to know this stranger who had let me be bombed in Germany while she, according to some photographs, had lived in the lap of luxury here, without a care in the world. (Well... one can't tell much from a photograph taken at the World's Fair.) Everyone looked posh there in their Sunday best. When she said "My son!" I wanted to cry and laugh at the same time. What did she know about her son? What nerve she had to call me that. But there was nothing that could be said or done to change things. My life was about to take a new turn.

Mr. Mitchell was there with his car to bring me to my new home in Bedford Stuyvesant. What a strange place this was. It seemed a very mysterious world. Everything was so different and there was no rubble in the street and no look of a war-torn area.

What a shock it was to me as I learned that we were the only white family within miles. All the other people were browns of various shades, and, to me, they all looked the same. It would take months for me to adjust my seeing so that I could tell the ladies apart when they stopped in to do their shopping for the weekend meals.

This mother became my mom, and the invalid, suffering from heart problems, became my pop. Mom was a very energetic woman and worked long hours in the store. After all the customers had finished shopping for the day, there was all the clean up to be done. I often helped her in the store. At first, I could not communicate with anyone because I spoke no English, and nobody else spoke German. For several years, my mother tried to keep me out of sight from her customers. She probably had not thought about how she was going to explain me to them. She was vague what she told them. Sometimes she would say that I had been away "in the countryside" or "at school." Anyway, she must have thought it was none of their business. However, it amused me when I finally understood what was going on.

In addition to all these new dynamics was the fact that I now was no longer an only child; I had a sister, Helen. She was older and knew nothing about my previous incarnation in Germany. So there was no understanding between us. She forbade me to speak in German, never wanted to know anything about Germany, and never went there. She had no interest in my previous life. It was a lonely time for me. It was hard to be me, and I was not sure who I was now in this new world. While formerly I was a member of a village community, now I was

Pokrajina Slovenija.
Provincia Sloveniae.

Skofija Ljubljanska.
Dioecesis Labacensis.

Štev. *9*
Num.

Rojstni in krstni list. — Testimonium nativitatis et baptismi.

Iz rojstne in krstne knjige župnije (duhovnije) *Draga*
Extractus e libro natorum et baptizatorum parochiae

Zvezek *IV* stran *187* štev. *20*
Tomus pagina numerus

Draga

Leto, mesec in dan Annus, mensis, dies	rojstva nativitatis	~~29. 3. 1901~~
	krsta baptismi	*31. 3. 1901*
Kraj rojstva (ulica) h. št. Locus nativitatis		*Podpreska štev. 1*
Ime otrokovo Nomen infantis		*Emilija*
Zakonski, nezakonski, sin, hči Legitimus, illegitimus, filius, filia		*zakonska hči*
Krstno in rod- binsko ime, stan in vera	očeta patris	*Janez Turk, kremljak*
Nomen, cognomen, conditio, religio	matere matris	*Ana Mihelič*
Krstno in rodbinsko ime, stan botrov Patrini		*Lorenc Cimprič*
		Marija Turk
Krstitelj Baptizans		*Tomaž Žabukovec, žup. upr.*

V dokaz resničnosti lastnoročni podpis in uradni pečat.
In quorum fidem subscriptio manu propria et sigillum officii.

Župni urad
Ex .officio parochiali *v Dragi 21. 1. 1924.*

Franc Goncar

Kolek in taksa
Bol. cum taxa

St. 19. Jugoslovanska knjigarna, Ljubljana.

6379 33

Mother's baptismal certificate

a lone individual in an alien world, with one heck of a hardworking mother.

When it came to going to school, my mother wanted me to be in a school where I at least had some white students to whom I could relate. She petitioned the Board of Education to allow me to attend Halsey Junior High. She knew little about schools, but she knew what she wanted and she got it. That was a behavior that I learned from her, yet I am not sure I applied that behavior as well or as often as she did. Later in life, I thought of her as having been a soldier in her manner of living. I thought she fought for what she believed in and what she thought was her due. When she died, I bought a soldier's wreath with laurel leaves and yellow roses like a corsage on its side.

Me as a young man in New York.

Here I am on a summer trip back to Germany with Uncle Ottmar and an East-German refugee who came to live in Hausa for a while.

Mama Karolina in old age.

ABOUT THE AUTHOR

Karl J. Volk was born in Brooklyn, New York in 1932. However, because of the arrival of the Great Depression and family circumstances, he was sent to Germany when only eleven- months old, where he spent his formative years living with his paternal uncles and their wives in Holzkirhausen and Aschaffenburg. It wasn't long after he moved there that Adolph Hitler came to power, and Karl's education included growing up in Nazi Germany as a "watched" American.

Karl's interest in art was sparked by living, for a time, in the same house as Mr. Adalbert Hock, a well-known artist who painted altar pieces and scenes of Aschaffenburg. Karl was intrigued after meeting with the artist. He returned to the United States in 1946, about a year after World War II ended. His growing interest in art continued, and he graduated from Brooklyn College in 1955 with a B.A. in Art Education.

After his schooling, Karl began a teaching career in various school districts in upstate New York. His longest and final tenure was in the Spackenkill School District of Poughkeepsie, lasting over twenty-five years. He has also lectured and conducted classes for adults in community programs and is the curator for the Unitarian Universalist Fellowship of Poughkeepsie. He would like to establish an Art Repository, a place where artwork from Senior artists can be cleanly and securely stored—in a climate-safe location—to be viewed and purchased upon request, and be available as a teaching and exploratory lesson for future artists, visitors, and friends.

Since the Covid-19 pandemic hit the United States in early 2020, Karl has been focusing on donating his paintings and other works of art to first responders working in area hospitals. You can see his work and contact him through his website at karljvolkstudios@yolasite.com.

www.ingramcontent.com/pod-product-compliance
Lightning Source LLC
Chambersburg PA
CBHW022032090426
42741CB00007B/1028